Table of Contents

Contents

Contents

Contents

Introduction

Whether it takes the form of physical violence or verbal or online harassment, bullying can have serious and lasting effects. In this book, teens write about these effects from the perspective of victim, bully and, in some cases, both.

Teens who are bullied often bear the burden on their own and end up feeling isolated and depressed. In "Feeling Different," author Isiah Van Brackle shuts himself off from his peers as a form of self-defense. The anonymous author of "Fortress of Solitude" retreats from her family after enduring years of teasing. It's only when they finally reach out to someone that the authors begin to heal.

Some teens react to bullying by becoming aggressive themselves. In "I Showed My Enemies—And Hurt My Friends, Too," author Elie Elius becomes combative to protect himself from bullying. It works, but he ends up alienating himself from his friends as well as his tormenters. And in "The Walking Flame," Eric Green begins to push people away—sometimes literally—to stay safe from bullies. But now as a young adult, he sometimes finds himself overreacting to the people he cares about.

Others take this line of defense a step further, becoming bullies themselves. "Since people didn't like me, I thought I might as well give them a reason," writes the anonymous author of "Bad Boy Gets a Conscience." He becomes a bully after getting picked on as a child. When he decides to give himself a personality make-over, he has to learn how to let down his guard and connect with his peers for the first time.

In "Releasing My Rage" and "Vicious Cycles," Miguel Ayala also writes about picking on his peers after he is tormented nearly everywhere he goes—at home, at school, and in his group home. His interview with therapist Jonathan Cohen sheds some light on why victims of bullying often become bullies themselves.

"No one likes to feel helpless," says Cohen. Bullying someone can make a teen who has been abused or bullied feel powerful for a brief moment.

Cohen also warns that adults often underestimate how harmful bullying is. Both victim and bully are at risk for depression, and bullying can lead to more violent behavior. In the last story in the book, "How Adults Can Help," Miguel passes on some of Cohen's tips for how adults can intervene and help stop bullying.

In the meantime, teens can take comfort in the words of some young writers who have experienced bullying firsthand. In their stories, victims of bullying show not only how damaging this often-overlooked form of violence can be, but also the steps they took to get help and feel better. And writers who have been the bullies reveal themselves in a way that will give readers a better understanding of this pattern of violence that harms both victim and perpetrator.

In some stories, names and identifying details have been changed.

Shaun Shishido

Fashion Un-Conscious

By Nadishia Forbes

Back home in Jamaica, I never worried about whether my clothes matched. At school, the only thing that mattered was how clean my uniform was and whether it was ironed. When I went to visit my friends, I would just put on a couple of freshly washed pieces of clothing without even thinking about how they looked.

We were kids—our friendships were not based on appearance; we just liked to run around and have fun. It didn't matter if our braided hair was pointing in all directions and our blouses and skirts had some buttons missing, or if we were barefoot and covered in red dirt.

I never experienced being judged because of the way I dressed—until I came to the U.S. The first time it happened was on my first day of junior high school, which was also my first day in an American school.

I was a little scared that day, mainly because of the new environment. Walking down the hall, I felt very self-conscious, so I turned around to get a better look at my classmates.

Two girls were staring at me, whispering and giggling. I stopped and waited for them to pass, but they said to go ahead, so I did. They continued looking at me, but I didn't say anything because I didn't know how to respond.

Even though I couldn't hear their conversation, I assumed it had something to do with the way I was dressed. They were wearing designer jeans, the latest name brand sneakers, and outfits that matched. Plus, they had their hair permed.

I never experienced being judged because of the way I dressed—until I came to the U.S.

I was wearing a pink and black plaid jumper with two straps in front, a blue, red, and white striped long-sleeved blouse, thick black stockings, and brown shoes. And I just had big braids in my hair, because my grandmother didn't want me to perm it, and that was fine with me.

When I got to my first period class, a couple or more of my classmates pointed out my shoes or clothes to their friends and laughed. Some of them even started throwing papers in my direction.

I looked different than everyone else and that was a big problem. When you start junior high, the pressure to fit in and gain respect is intense. The kids who made fun of me were popular—partly because their designer clothes made them seem cool. My clothes made me stand out and gave the others an excuse to pick on me.

I was the perfect target and it wasn't just because of the way I dressed. I was in a new environment and that made me feel scared and insecure. I was like a fish outside its water bowl. My classmates saw that I was in a position of weakness and wouldn't stand up for myself. They took advantage of that.

Almost every day, I would be greeted with giggles, pointing, and other demonstrations of their disapproval. For a long time, I didn't have any friends to back me up and the teacher did nothing to control the students. I felt like everyone was against me, like no one was on my side. Two girls named Luvia and Nefertiti were the main sources of my torment. They would put "kick me" signs on my back, throw papers at me and make fun of my clothes.

For the first time in my life, I didn't want to go to school. When I got home each day, I would cry and complain to my grandmother about what was happening, but she was too busy to do anything about it. Sometimes she would say, "Ignore them," or tell me to tell their mothers. Then she would force me to go back to school. She never really understood how hurt and depressed I was.

I would go to school each day with my heart pounding. I hardly paid attention and I never really learned anything. It was hard to concentrate on my schoolwork. The other students were very disruptive. Because I was quiet, the teacher always pointed me out as an example to the rest of the class and that made it worse for me because I was now considered the teacher's pet.

To take my mind off the fact that I might end up in a fight any minute, I'd bring a thick romance novel to school and just sit in class and read all day. Instead of focusing on learning like I should have, I focused on surviving.

I did make one friend that year. Her name was Tina. She was really friendly and we had a couple of things in common. We were both from Jamaica, but Tina had been here for five years. We both had strict families. Tina wore the latest styles of name brand clothing, just like Luvia and Nefertiti, but unlike them, she never judged me for the way I dressed.

Tina would take up for me when the others were picking on me. She would tell them to leave me alone and always tried to help me out. One time, Luvia tried to spite Tina by saying that

Tina and I were sisters. Later that day, I wrote a poem to Tina, titled, "You're Like a Sister," and she liked it.

Having Tina as a friend made the days more bearable because I was not entirely alone. But it didn't make much of a difference in terms of how I was treated by the other kids. In fact, it didn't make any difference at all.

Around the middle of the school term, I started to think that maybe if I dressed like the rest of them, they wouldn't bother me so much. I hadn't made any effort to fit in sooner because I was stubborn. But I was tired of having people treat me like I was beneath them.

Instead of focusing on learning like I should have, I focused on surviving.

One day, I went to school wearing yellow socks and a yellow blouse with a black skirt. Right at the beginning of class, Nefertiti showed Luvia my socks and said, "What are you doing?" with a smirk. It was as if she was saying, "No matter what you do, you won't look as good as us." Not knowing what to say, I turned my back, feeling a little defeated. I went back to wearing my usual outfits.

A month or two later, my uncle's girlfriend gave me a pair of trendy sneakers. I wore them to school and I have to admit they gave me a little confidence. I actually felt some enthusiasm, thinking that probably I would get a little acceptance with my new shoes.

When I got to school, one kid actually announced to the class that I had on name brand sneakers. Everyone looked, but I didn't feel any more accepted by my peers than I had before.

No matter what I did, they wouldn't let up. Luvia, in particular, was always throwing things at me or hitting me. I never started anything with her; she was always coming after me. Then the kids she hung around with would tell her how bad she was.

One day in the spring, she was in the hallway surrounded by her friends when I passed by. When she saw me, she hit me. I didn't want to fight, so I continued to walk, as I usually did. But for some reason on that day, I couldn't take it anymore. I decided it had to stop.

So when I saw Luvia in the cafeteria, I went up to her and slapped her face. The next thing I knew, I was on the floor. Luvia was much bigger than me so it wasn't much of a surprise when I lost the fight.

Later that day, Luvia and her friends came up to me. She was very upset and kept staring at me, but she didn't say anything. I went home early.

That night, I told my father how these two girls had been giving me a hard time. He decided to take a day off from work and come to school with me and make a complaint. We went to the counselor's office. She called in Luvia, sat the two of us down, and asked about the fight and about what was going on between us. Then she talked to us for a while.

I didn't really hear what the counselor was saying. I was too busy staring at Luvia and wondering what she thought about all this and what the other kids would think when they heard about it. After my father left, I went back to class. Everyone was looking at me.

After that, Luvia didn't hit me or throw things at me anymore but she and her friends still gave me dirty looks.

When I finally finished 7th grade, I had the greatest summer of my life—simply because I had survived. I would stay home most of the time watching TV, without anyone tormenting me.

In 8th grade, things got better. Everyone started to settle in and feel more comfortable. They let down some of their guard, which made for a less hostile environment. My classmates stopped making fun of my clothes. I didn't really change the way I dressed, but I stopped wearing certain things—like skirts and dresses that made me look like I was going to church.

I got the chance to make more friends because everyone was friendlier. When I got the chance to know my classmates, I was surprised. They weren't really bad people. And Luvia and Nefertiti weren't in my class anymore, which made everything much easier for me. I didn't dread going to school anymore.

Seventh grade was a difficult year, but I got through it, I think because I knew it wouldn't always be that way and I was determined to succeed. My family and Tina did their best to help me, but the strength I had inside came from my faith in God.

That experience taught me never to judge people by appearance. I never tease anyone because of what they wear or how they look. I've also got the best of friends because I didn't pick them based on how they look, but by getting to know them as individuals.

After 7th grade, I only saw Nefertiti and Luvia occasionally. But, during graduation rehearsal, I saw Luvia giggling and whispering to her friend and I could tell they were talking about me.

It didn't bother me at all. Knowing that this was the end of 8th grade and junior high and that I would never have to see them again, I gave them a big smile. And that wiped the smile off Luvia's face. I think she was disappointed because I wasn't upset. She no longer had any power over me. I turned around feeling happy and triumphant.

I'm in 11th grade now and I don't get teased anymore, even though I still dress pretty much the same way. I have friends now. I know that I'm smart and will be successful one day. But the difficulty I went through in 7th grade still has an effect on me.

Sometimes, when I walk in front of the class, I feel self-conscious about my appearance. Sometimes, when I hear someone laughing, I still think they're laughing at me.

Nadishia was 17 when she wrote this story.
She later joined the Army.

Paul John Paredes

I Showed My Enemies—
And Hurt My Friends, Too

By Elie Elius

To the reader:

As you read this story, there will be certain stuff I did that you will not be so happy about. But if you had been in my shoes, you might have felt differently.

I am proud of the way I used to act toward my so-called friends, the ones who picked on me all the time. It was good for me to learn to stand up for myself. But what I am not proud of is the way I acted toward those who cared.

Like a turtle, I built a strong shell to protect myself from the insults. But those who cared were getting shell-shocked also. Only, I didn't notice until they all started to leave.

When I came to America from Haiti, I was very shy and passive. I was in a new country, I was the new kid on the block, and

I was desperate to be liked. The best way I could make friends, I thought, was to fit in with the crowd. I used to let my so-called friends walk all over me because I was afraid that if I spoke up, they wouldn't want to be seen with me.

They told me I was down and I could hang with them, but later on I found out they were using me as a big joke. Phrases like, "You hear the way that n-gga talk!" or, "He looks so ugly and retarded," were constantly being thrown at me at home and at school.

I did not know English well and people would make fun of the way I spoke. Their words would sizzle on my skin like butter hitting a hot skillet. Plus, back in the day, my head used to be bigger than my body and a person couldn't tell me from a brown toothpick. All of these flaws added me up to laughter and jokes.

Their words would sizzle on my skin like butter hitting a hot skillet.

Just for the hell of it, one of my friends would say, "Your father left you 'cause he didn't want your ugly ass."

My father the deadbeat left my mother before I was born, and my so-called friend had no idea why he flew out on us. Still, just hearing him say those words made me feel hurt and angry.

I felt their words strike my heart like a sharp, pointy spear. I felt like dirt under their shoes that they could just wipe off. And, from around the time I was 9 till I was about 12, it went on and on. But then I began to decide that enough was enough.

No, I didn't wake up one morning and say, "OK, no more." But slowly, as I got older, I decided that I was tired of coming home from school crying. I was sick of avoiding my cousins, who also made fun of me, hiding out in the kitchen if they were in my living room.

Reader, what would you do if you were constantly being picked on?

When I talked to people I was close to, they would say, "Pay them jerks no mind. Keep your head up at all times." When I came home depressed, my mother would sometimes say, "People picked on me all the time. Just ignore their talk."

But I could not ignore it and I did not know how to keep my head up. If I wanted this foul treatment to stop I would either have to a) run away, 'cause I knew my mother would not move just because I was getting picked on, or b) change my attitude and start wiping people off of me. I chose b.

C hange is a hard path to cross in life. Sometimes it is for the better; sometimes it is for the worse. Who really knows? Maybe the person who is doing the morphing does not know himself.

The good point for me was that I let a lot of people know I was not going to take their crap. The bad point was that I lost a lot of good people by being all hard. Still, the first time I really stood up for myself took a lot of courage, and I'm glad I did it.

One day, this dumb kid in my school went up to the board when the teacher was not there and started drawing me as a stick figure with mean little details. One of my so-called friends found this so amusing he just had to join in. Of course, the whole class was laughing and pointing at me, and I felt like a rag.

At first I just went up and asked them if they could stop making fun of me because I didn't like it. Then my friend began to mock me and that other kid pushed me. I went back to my seat but they were still up there laughing, and the other kids were pointing and laughing also. At that moment I couldn't take it.

I remembered my uncle saying that if you want to get through to people, you have to be aggressive. So I stood up, walked in front of the class and erased my picture. Where on earth did that courage come from? I have no idea, but I'm glad it came.

"What's your problem, you a-hole?" the kid asked me.

I said, "@#%&* you."

It was right there and then I got into my first fight. My friend punched me in my face and the other kid just kept on punching me in the stomach. Even though I lost, this incident began the whole "Don't mess with me" sitcom. After that, I began to be more and more aggressive.

I didn't change overnight. I just always had that new attitude in my mind and as time flowed, I began to pick up a few bad habits here and there. After a while I became a foul-mouthed little brat, and phrases like "lick my balls" and "just like your dog-face mother" would roll off my tongue with fire.

I did not go around spitting venom at everyone, just on the fools who messed with me. And of course I wasn't all mouth. I had a little action also, and sometimes I'd get into fights.

Day by day, my demons began to go bye-bye. People stopped picking on me and I had this feeling that I had accomplished something big. Infamy became me. The problem was that in some ways, I began to act different with just about everybody—not just my so-called friends, but my real friends, too.

At any little thing someone did to me, even if it was just a friendly joke, I would snap or get ready to fight. Lots of times when I probably didn't need to, I kept my distance and had my guard up.

Plus, if I was hurt, I wouldn't talk to my friends about what was going on. I'd cut them out or get into a fight. That's how I lost my friend Syretta (not her real name).

I remember her party like I remember my mother's name.

Syretta was one of my best and most trusted friends. She understood me and what I was going through. I could really talk to her about my problems and feelings. I loved her like a sister.

But for her 13th birthday, she invited some friends to her house for her party and didn't invite me. Syretta and I never had any beef that I knew about, so I was upset. I did not want to go up to her and ask her what was going on because I felt embarrassed.

So on the night of the party, I went uninvited. When I saw my friend Rafael, I went over to talk to him about Syretta. Rafael and I were not as close as I was with Syretta. We just played sports and chilled. But he was another person I could trust.

"You know that fat b-tch did not invite me. What she got with me anyway?" I said.

I guess someone might have overheard what I said because a couple of minutes later Syretta's mother came in my face.

"I will really appreciate it if you would leave my home. I do not like or allow this kind of rudeness in my house," she said.

I was so outraged that I actually went up to Rafael and punched him because I thought he was the one who told Syretta what I'd said. When I did this, everyone stopped and looked at me with disgust. Syretta's father called my mother. Then he dragged me out of his house.

At the time I was just angry. But now I feel ashamed. I was cursing and carrying on like I had no type of home training. And I feel bad, because even

People stopped picking on me and I had this feeling that I had accomplished something big.

though I still don't understand why Syretta didn't invite me to her party, she really had been a good friend and I messed up our friendship.

I see Rafael sometimes but it is just a hi-bye thing. And as for Syretta, I have not heard from her since that dreadful party. When I look back at the way I acted, I won't apologize for everything I did. It's important to stand up for yourself. In this world, if you want the honey, you have to kill a few bees.

Still, sometimes I kind of regret the way I carried myself. All that big and bad stuff wasn't me. I never wanted to go around attacking people like a pit bull. Times change and so do people. All that be-my-friend and I-don't-like-you crap is for elementary school, and that is where I left it.

When I went into high school, I decided I had to act and carry myself differently. I decided that when I entered the school building, I entered for an education, not to be liked, because looking for friends is what got me into this garbage in the first place.

At first I stuck by myself. But soon I found that people were coming up to me and wanting to be my friend, probably because I was just being myself.

I'm not a punk, so if fighting is the only way to solve a problem, OK. But I don't go to extremes, and I don't let that tough way be the only way I deal with my problems anymore.

Now if I have a problem or conflict, most often I will try to talk things through. Plus, now I know who my real friends are. They are giving me something that I gave but did not receive before: respect.

Elie was 16 when he wrote this story.

Ogen Dolma

The Walking Flame

By Eric Green

As a little kid, I was feisty, but I did not have to look for trouble.
Trouble came looking for me.

I was in elementary school the first time I was bullied. I was
doing my schoolwork when a student threw something at me.
I looked back to see who threw it, then went back to doing my
work. First warning. When the student did it again, I said to
myself, "Oh, hell no!" I got up from my seat and shoved that student against the wall. I said, "You wanna mess with me?" Second
warning. He stopped.

But the bullying never let up. When I moved from Long
Island to the Bronx, I was teased because I was smart and because
of the way I looked. I was a geek. Yes, I had on those tight-ass
pants, suspenders, a tight long-sleeved shirt and big glasses. If
you saw me then, you'd be like, "Eric, you look like Steve Urkel!

You look like a nerd!" Well, based on how I looked, I was humiliated by the whole school. It was not pretty.

When I entered junior high, I thought the bullying would be over. Wrong! But that year I decided there was no way in hell I was going out like a sucker. I had to let these bullies know that I could fight back. I started kicking and pushing anyone who touched me.

I wish I did not have to be the walking flame, always pushing people away just to be safe.

I remember when a student who looked like a punk tried it with me. He pushed me against the wall. Then all of my strength rushed through my hands and I pushed him back with full force. He fell backwards and slipped on a big puddle of milk that sent him flying across the lunchroom.

"See, that's what you get when you mess with me, sucker," I said. I thought he would quit it, but the principal had to break up the fight.

High school was only worse. My personality changed. Remember Dr. Jekyll and Mr. Hyde? Well, I was like that. I could not take one bit of harassment. I became the "walking flame," warning people not to mess with me. Any time someone spoke to me I was ready to go off.

I got a little paranoid. I even began to feel as if the teachers were bullying me. "Oh, that's just great. Just dandy," I said to myself if a teacher asked something simple like, "Where's your homework?" The way I saw it, they were just harassing me.

My art teacher once said, "You're just like an old man, so rigid!"

"Why did you call me rigid?" I said loudly. "I'm not like an old man. I don't like to do things I don't want to do. I am what I am, and you're gonna have to deal with it whether you like it or not!" I was furious.

"Calm down, Eric. Don't be so sensitive," the teacher said.

During high school, I was bullied more and more because I was gay. Students approached me with personal questions—sometimes out of curiosity, other times to humiliate me. Sometimes it felt like being bullied was all I would experience in life.

Finally, I switched to an alternative school where the other students and teachers were much more accepting of my sexuality and my ways. Even so, it's taken me years to stop feeling like I'm being constantly pushed around and harassed. I was even furious with my mother many times when I felt like she was bullying me.

When I look back on what I went through, I get very upset. I hate that feeling of powerlessness that I have been carrying for a very long time. For years I felt as if I deserved to be bullied because as a child I had nothing. I wasn't taken care of by my parents, and I didn't get much attention from my family or my foster families. I believed bullies picked on me because they saw that I was somebody who could not defend himself and had no one in life to defend him.

I wonder what I would be like now if I hadn't been bullied. How would I be different if I didn't have to watch my back when I went to class or didn't have to worry about being picked on while I was trying to figure out my sexual orientation? How would I have grown if I'd had more friends and could've taken the chance to be more of myself?

I wish I did not have to be the walking flame, always pushing people away just to be safe. The habit I developed of defending myself constantly has definitely affected my friendships. Sometimes I see teasing but helpful criticism as a form of bullying. My feelings get hurt all the time.

I sometimes don't realize that I'm overreacting because even constructive criticism rubs me wrong. Then people say, "I'm just trying to help!"

I feel so confused. I can't tell anymore if I'm being too sensitive or my friends are being too insensitive. Either way, the past bullying causes a lot of problems between me and the people close to me. Day to day, I still worry that someone will start harassing me for no reason, and that the terrible feelings of my childhood will come back to me at any time.

But sometimes it's not my imagination. Even though I'm 23, I still get nasty comments, usually about my sexuality. They still have the power to make my self-esteem sink to the bottom and make me feel like I'm nothing. When people harass me on the street, I sometimes wonder, "If I fought back in the past, why is it hard for me to fight back now?"

But I am older and don't want to fight anymore. I've learned that fighting doesn't solve the problem. So I just try to keep walking, and I say to myself, "Eric, those bullies are not worth your time."

Eric was 23 when he wrote this story.

Anaïs Ngo Nsang

Fortress of Solitude

By Anonymous

One day in 5th grade, a boy came and sat next to me in the cafeteria during lunch. Before I could react, he took my pizza from me and threw it in my face for no apparent reason. I got up and chased him around the cafeteria, trying to ignore the cackling and hurtful remarks like "ugly girl" and "dummy" coming from the other kids. This wasn't the first time I'd had to defend myself against my classmates.

When I was in elementary school, I didn't really have friends because I was shy and quiet and I focused on being a proper student. Most of the other kids in my school disrespected teachers and misbehaved. Starting in 2nd grade, my classmates took it upon themselves to bully, tease, and totally humiliate me.

They would hit me and call me degrading names like stupid, crazy girl, and b-tch. I was always anxious because I thought that

29

every kid in my school had it in for me. My acting like a scared animal around them only caused them to torment me even more.

But when I told the teacher a kid had hit me, they would wait until after class to punish the kid, or they wouldn't do anything at all. I began to feel as though I was on my own to defend myself. I thought of myself as a weak person because I felt it was my job to stop the bullying and I couldn't. I felt vulnerable and alone.

Luckily, even though school was bad, I always had another place to cheer me up: home. At home, I felt safe and invincible, like an impenetrable fortress that could never be brought down. My parents and three sisters accepted me for who I was.

But even so, I didn't tell my family what was happening, because I felt it was my job to watch my own back. If I was quiet and they asked what was wrong, I would just get anxious and say, "Nothing," even though I wanted to say how bad I was feeling inside.

As the bullying continued over the years, I grew more distant from my parents and sisters. I still talked to them, but only short talks about my day. Somehow, they knew that I was having some kind of trouble at school without me having to tell them. They told me not to be phased by it and to ignore it. But it was already too late for that.

I thought of myself as weak, because I felt it was my job to stop the bullying and I couldn't.

I could see they were worried about me and I felt guilty because I thought I was a burden to them. After school I began going straight to my room, isolating myself from the rest of the family. I didn't want them to know how bad things were at school. Unfortunately, it eventually managed to reach home.

In 6th grade, due to the constant bullying and my rapid decrease in self-esteem, my grades took a turn for the worse. My parents started to lecture me that I could do better than this. I wanted nothing more than to tell them why my grades had dropped and why I had become distant from them, but I thought they would just pass it off as a pitiful excuse and yell at me even more. I was convinced that nobody would understand what was happening to me, so I kept the problem to myself.

Meanwhile, the stress of school and home was taking its toll on me. I felt like I was going to break any second. Then I became suicidal. I felt that since I couldn't talk to anybody, I would end my own life. I thought that maybe my parents and sisters wouldn't care if I killed myself because I wasn't acting like my usual self anymore. I thought that everyone would be better off without me. I pictured myself with a knife aimed at my wrists or my throat. I was planning to do it when nobody was around to stop me.

But then I thought about how my suicide would impact my family. Deep down, I knew that my family really did care about me. After a few months of thinking about suicide, I also knew I needed to share my feelings with someone.

I'm still not sure why, but I was afraid if I talked to my parents, they would think I was exaggerating. So instead, I told my 6th grade teacher that I needed to talk to her. I sat down nervously and she asked what was wrong.

"All the kids in school treat me as though I'm their play toy. They tease, hit and make fun of me. It's been happening for years now," I said. After that, I told her that I couldn't take it anymore and I wanted to commit suicide. At this point, I was crying and I was nervous about her reaction.

Her eyes widened, her eyebrows and face were perked in a worried manner. She took me to the psychiatrist on the first floor. He told me to sit down and then my teacher left the room to give us privacy. I got scared and wanted to leave, but I knew that if I did, my feelings would stay bottled up like a sealed jar of pickles.

It was silent in the room except for the sound of kids playing outside at recess. Then the psychiatrist broke the silence and said, "Everything will be OK. Just tell me what you said. It won't leave this room. However, if it's something serious like you planning to hurt yourself or others, or if it's abuse at home, I'll have to get you help."

That's when I got really nervous because I thought that by help, he meant putting me in a strait jacket and hauling me off to the crazy house like they did on TV. But I needed to get my feelings out and in the open. So I told him the same thing that I'd told my teacher.

After that, he called my home and told my mother to come up to the school as soon as she could. In less than 10 minutes she was there, sitting across from me with a worried look on her face.

Therapy taught me some ways to face school with a new attitude.

I stared at the floor for a long time, struggling with what I wanted to say to her. I'd been hiding these feelings for such a long time. I was scared that I was going to be sent off to a psychiatric facility for the rest of my life.

Finally, I said, "I feel like I can't talk to anybody about how I feel. I...I feel like committing suicide. Maybe if I do, then my family wouldn't have to deal with me." Tears began to flow from my eyes and I was shaking. I waited for my mother to say something. It was the longest wait of my entire life.

Wiping tears from her eyes, she said, "Sweetheart, you should have told us how you were feeling. We could have helped you with your problems. You should never have kept those feelings inside for this long. They could cause damage to you. You know that you can always come to us when you need help. I don't understand why this was any different."

To me, this situation felt different because the problem was in school. If the problem had been at home, I would have asked for help. But somehow I felt that since I was the one getting bullied, it was my fault and I should deal with it.

Later that afternoon, my mom took me to the hospital for a psychiatric evaluation. To tell the truth, I wasn't scared to go to the hospital anymore. I was happy that I had gotten it off of my chest.

At the hospital, a small woman with short hair and light skin sat down beside me and asked me why I felt suicidal. I told her about how I was always being bullied and teased in school, how I distanced myself from my family and bottled up my emotions. I felt that I wasn't good enough for my parents and that I would never exceed their expectations no matter how hard I tried. I felt insignificant and isolated from my own family and I didn't want to feel that way anymore.

The doctor told me that she had some problems when she was young, too. She said that people made fun of her head because it was the shape of a coconut. But she ignored them and focused on her own goals and people eventually stopped bothering her. She told me that if I have a goal that I want to reach, then I should just focus on that. Her words made me I felt like I wasn't alone anymore—there were people out there like me.

I started meeting with a therapist every other Thursday. The more I talked about my problems, the more I felt at ease with myself. My dad took me to my sessions and afterwards, he would ask how they went or I would tell him about them myself. Day by day, I started opening up to my family and spending time with them like I used to do. I could tell that they were happy to see me regaining my confidence, because they often had a surprised smile on their faces.

I was determined to do better in school because I wanted to regain a part of me that I lost during the bullying. I was fueled by the thought that I'd prove the bullies wrong and set them straight after years of being humiliated. Therapy taught me some ways to face school with a new attitude. I learned to breathe deeply to calm my nerves and to tell myself something encouraging each day, like, "Don't let them get to you" or, "I can make it."

One day during school, one of my classmates kept calling me names and poking me in the side. I didn't say anything or get upset. Instead, I ignored him and kept doing my work. The teacher turned around and yelled at him, which made him stop. After that, the kids in my class didn't bother me as much as before. I felt happy knowing that the therapy seemed to be helping me to stay calm when I was picked on.

But things really changed once I graduated from my elementary school after 8th grade. In high school I was able to start over fresh in a place where no one knew that I was a target. I found people who had a lot in common with me and began making some good friends. By the middle of 9th grade I was feeling so much better that I stopped going to therapy.

There are things that I'm still struggling with, like my anxiety. I still feel nervous most of the time, about things like my grades, and asking for help if I need it, and walking through crowded hallways in between classes.

At home, I'm still afraid to talk to my family sometimes and when I feel like I want to be alone, I hide out in my room for an hour or two listening to music, reading, or napping. Then my family steps in and tries to get me to spend more time with them like I used to.

It makes me sad to know that my family misses the old me. I miss the old me, too.

I miss the feeling of wanting to spend time with my family. I don't like feeling nervous, isolating myself in my room all the time and watching dust bunnies roll on the floor. I miss the fun, outgoing and carefree person that I used to be when I was little. I'm not sure how to get back to that person, but I'm trying.

The author was 16 when she wrote this story.

Gamal Jones

Feeling Different

By Isiah Van Brackle

It was a brisk day. The wind was blowing semi-dried leaves, signaling the death of summer vacation's freedom and the rebirth of the oppressions of school. In the schoolyard, the other 4th graders were talking with their friends.

I stood alone on the sidelines, praying no one would see me and I could finally have a normal year, even if that meant staying free of human contact.

Memories of the previous year were still fresh in my head. Memories of going hungry because my lunch was stolen, memories of stinging pain, warm saliva sliding down my cheek, and the sickening feeling of helplessness.

Unfortunately, the school bully took that moment to interrupt my walk down memory lane so that he could reintroduce himself. "Man, there are too many girls in this school. I think something should be done about it, don't you?" he asked me with a deadly edge to his voice.

I remained silent, glancing around nervously for the help I knew wouldn't be coming.

"Yeah, too many girls like you in this school, and it's up to people like me to resolve it," he said, pulling back his hand and balling it into a tight fist.

RRIINNGG! "Yes!" I thought. "Saved by th—" My thoughts were cut short as his fist slammed into my stomach, knocking the air out of my lungs.

I've felt different for as long as I can remember, like something at the core of my humanity is missing, separating me from everyone else. Growing up, the feeling was always there, even around family members. Though they were never judgmental, I trusted them as much as everyone else—not at all.

Although I craved human connection like any other kid, I had no idea how to interact with people, so I stayed away from them. My mother says that when I was little, she'd ask me why I wasn't playing with the other kids at the park, and I'd respond, "Because I don't know if they're good or bad." But I've always felt that what separated me from everyone was much deeper than that.

When I reached elementary school, I didn't know what other children my age liked to do, or the popular terms and phrases they used. That led to me getting tormented by other kids, and I began to feel that I wasn't worth the time to understand or love.

It got to the point where the only time I interacted with other kids was when they hit me, spit on me, stole from me, or threw my books (and sometimes me) into garbage cans.

When I went on to junior high school, things improved slightly, but not enough. The only people I made friends with were a few older girls. Unlike most guys my age, they could talk about things besides sex and dating, like life and our futures.

But being friends with them just made matters worse. They'd defend me whenever they could, and then when they weren't around, my tormentors would return and say, "Your girlfriends aren't here to protect you," as they proceeded to make up for all the harassment they'd missed.

Finally, I decided I'd had enough. But instead of fighting back physically, I decided to protect myself by cutting myself off from my emotions.

After that, whenever I did feel some spark of sadness or anger, it didn't matter to me anymore. Once I became indifferent, my tormentors discovered it wasn't fun to bully me anymore and they stopped. But I still felt alone.

I had no idea how to interact with people, so I stayed away from them.

I began to watch people from a distance, trying to figure out what exactly made me so different. I observed people much like a scientist would. I watched their mannerisms and how their actions differed depending on who was around. I noticed things like an involuntary twitch or smirk that revealed what action a person was about to take.

After a while, I found that by just being near a person I could pick up on their emotions and use them to predict how a situation would turn out. I learned what to do or not do, what to say or not say, so that I could avoid conflict.

Once this ability came naturally to me, I found I was able to fit in with the emo and goth cliques because of my cynical nature and somewhat creepy way of not showing emotion. Still, I didn't connect with people. The relationships were all superficial.

I also found that once I started spending more time around other people and taking in all their emotions, I lost myself. I found it hard to distinguish my own emotions from those of everyone around me, and I felt overwhelmed.

Then, during freshman year of high school, I met a girl named Jade. She'd also had a rough past and we soon became close friends. Because I still appeared indifferent, Jade would often tease me to try to get me to react. I usually laughed at her attempts and told her it didn't bother me, until one day it did.

We were in the lunchroom and she started her usual routine: hitting, screaming, and throwing condiments at me. In doing so, she ruined my favorite shirt. I don't know why, but something snapped in me. She'd finally managed to hurt me inside. I didn't say anything, but the pain was clear on my normally impassive face. She looked upset and didn't speak to me the rest of that day.

My tormentors discovered it wasn't fun to bully me anymore and they stopped. But I still felt alone.

The next morning, I awoke to the sounds of thunder and walked to the bus stop in the pouring rain. The bus—when it finally came—wasn't much of a haven. Water seeped through the spaces between the windows, soaking me almost as much as the rain outside.

Two stops later, Jade got on the bus with a solemn look on her face—which was strange because she loved the rain—and sat next to me, as usual. She handed me a folded piece of paper and said, "There's no need to reply."

I unfolded it and found a letter of apology, the first apology I'd ever received.

For the first time in four years I had shown emotion, and for the first time I'd gotten a response, showing me how much someone cared. I called Jade a moron, claiming it wasn't that big a deal, but since then we've been closer than ever.

Jade also unwittingly gave me a way to filter out all the overwhelming emotions and seal them within paper: poetry. Jade writes poetry to convey her pain, and she soon introduced me to the art.

I've found that writing poetry is the only way to truly express myself without any barriers. The moon is a focal point in many of my poems. Whenever it's mentioned, I'm talking about myself. I compare myself to the moon because it's separate from the world, floating in a void of nothingness.

And while the moon may sometimes seem insignificant, it has the power to affect the nature of the world. That's the way I've always felt I was viewed—a child worth nothing, deemed emotionless, yet capable of so much more.

These days, I see myself in a sort of limbo—stable but fragile. I've made progress, and I do find comfort in my friend Jade and in my family and the few people I now trust, and so for the most part I'm OK. But sometimes the feeling of being lost and alone gets overwhelming. No one truly understands me, not even Jade.

I want to finally be truly understood. I've always wanted someone who'd love me and accept me for who I am. I want a sanctuary, a haven for everything I've ever felt—someone to finally contain my emotions—and I want to be able to do the same for them.

But first I need to learn to trust someone enough to get close to them, and it's hard to imagine that ever happening. It's difficult for me to get close to people because I still find their emotions so overwhelming.

Isiah was 15 when he wrote this story.

Learning to Love My Hair

By Charlene George

A few weeks after I was put in foster care, my foster mother told me I was going to get my hair cut. I was 7 years old, and I couldn't remember ever getting my hair cut before. I had no image of what it would look like.

We went into a Spanish hair salon, and I saw lots of happy people coming out. I was sitting there saying to myself, "I hope I am going to be one of those happy people." But when I saw people's hair falling to the floor, my chin dropped. I was scared.

"Come on baby, you're next," they said. They turned me to where I could not see the mirror. I could hear the scissors slapping towards my hair and I saw so much hair falling out. I was worried, asking, "Why do you have to cut so much hair?"

My foster mother told me to sit and be quiet. The man said, "Trust me, it's going to look nice."

When he finished, he turned my chair around and I looked in the mirror. I wanted to cry but I didn't want my foster mother to yell at me. It was too short—it only came halfway down my forehead. I was not very pleased, knowing it was too late now to take back my OK.

The other people waiting to get their hair done told me it looked nice. But I wasn't sure. I felt like a different person. The main thing on my mind was how all the people at school would react.

The next morning, I couldn't wait to get to school to see what everyone would think. I did my best with my hair and got on the bus. But then I started to feel nervous. I worried that the kids at my school were not going to like it.

A lot of people noticed my haircut, and one teacher told me how nice my hair looked. Then it happened. There was this group who thought they were so cool. They always had something bad to say about others to put them down. They'd say things like, "Look at that fat girl," or they'd make fun of someone for not having on some name brand clothes or sneakers.

As soon as they saw my new haircut they started laughing and saying mean things. I was so hurt. They had a lot of jokes for me, laughing and pointing their fingers.

I thought it was going to stop there, but it didn't. I hated having people judge me by my hair. They pointed at my head and called me bald, and even made a song about it at lunch.

I felt like a piece of bread that a whole lot of birds were trying to feed off of.

The song went something like: "You're a bald-headed chick-chick, you ain't got no hair in the back, gel up, weave up, your hair is messed up." It bothered me so much I would leave the lunchroom or my classroom and cry my heart out in the school bathroom.

Eventually, my hair started to grow out, but that didn't stop people from making fun of me. And whenever my foster mother decided I needed another haircut, I got one. I didn't have a choice.

I used to hate to feel myself break down when people were being negative about my hairstyle. It made me feel so down on myself that I started to believe I was ugly, that no one cared and that the world was against me. I felt like a piece of bread that a whole lot of birds were trying to feed off of.

I knew that the kids at school were not going to stop joking on me, so I had to plan something for myself to stop feeling the way I did.

For a while, I would try to fight back. I would make fun of how the other kids looked, too, like how one of the guys had birthmarks all over his head that looked like ringworm. I also did things like throw spitballs, curse people out or just fight.

Doing things like that made me feel better, but then I would get sent to the time out room or get suspended for a few days. I was going to start failing my classes if I didn't change my act.

One day I asked myself if I was really ugly like they said. My answer was no. I hadn't been ugly when my hair was long, so why should I be ugly now?

Telling myself I looked good and not ugly kept me feeling positive about myself, even when people made remarks.

I decided that I was not going to let the other kids provoke me into getting in trouble. I was going to choose the words that came out of my mouth wisely. I had to grow up and stop letting the things people said about me get to me.

Of course, that was easier said than done. It took me years to build up my confidence. But by the time I was around 16, I was ready to make some changes with my hair.

I knew I was getting more mature, so I wanted to try new looks. And I just wanted to feel cool for once. I started dying my hair and tried all different colors: black, light brown and dark brown, hazelnut, or orange mixed with red. I also put things in my hair like braids, and even some human hair. I even wore my hair short with wet-and-go curls at one point.

Sometimes other people liked my hair, and sometimes they didn't. But I was happy trying all those new hairstyles. And wearing my hair in ways that fit my body improved my self-esteem, even though I was still being bothered by other kids in school.

If I had a card for every day I was laughed at, I'd have a full deck, but I decided I was just going to have to let them play out. Sometimes I would still cry or I would tell them things like, "I'm still going to have a wonderful day," holding a smile when I said it. Telling myself I looked good and not ugly kept me feeling positive about myself, even when people made remarks.

Another thing that helped me were these two staff from the residential treatment center where I lived: Ms. Epps and Ms. Elliot. I looked up to them and thought of them as my stepmothers. They loved my hairstyles. They'd tell me my styles went with my features and made me look like an African princess. Listening to all the positive things they had to say made me feel better.

Now I'm 18, and when people bother me I try not to listen to them. I can feel that what's important is not what anyone else likes about me but what I like about myself. I've put in a lot of effort to feel comfortable with how I look.

Now I hold my head high and make sure my hair is looking fine. When people make comments I'll say something like, "God blessed me just like he will do for you, and have a blessed day."

They may look at me like I'm crazy and say they do not believe in God, but I just walk away and do not pay them any mind. Responding to mean comments by saying good things, or nothing at all, makes me feel happy.

These days I still change up my hairstyle a lot. I like making my own choices about how I look.

I sometimes go to the extreme, like when I cut all my hair off last summer, even shorter than what my foster mother did when I was 7 years old. I didn't really want to go bald, but my hair was falling out because of the chemicals and hair dyes I put in it.

But I worked my bald hair cut with confidence. I accessorized with a head scarf, and when people asked me why I cut my hair, I would just explain it to them and they understood.

I spent a long time beating myself up and not liking my hair just because someone else did not like it. It makes me feel good now to let everyone know that I am going to wear my hair however I want. Other people may like it or not, but I won't change it for anyone but me.

Charlene was 18 when she wrote this story.

Kenly Dillard/YC

Gay on the Block

By Jeremiyah Spears

Because I'm 6'6" and hefty, people often think I should be a ball-player of some sort. But once you get to know me, you'll know I'm no ballplayer.

In my old neighborhood, guys would always call me out of my house to play basketball, knowing that was not what I liked to do. When I missed a shot they would ridicule me and call me a faggot.

It's true, I'm gay, and though I look like your ordinary clean-cut Polo boy, I act a little feminine. When I'm happy, I like to buy shoes. I also like to read romances and family-oriented books. My favorite book is *Mama*, by Terry McMillan. It's about a divorced black woman with five kids who's having problems being accept-ed into society.

In fact, I've been different my whole life. I first realized I was homosexual at an early age. When I was around 5 or 6 years old, I would see boys and think, "How cute."

Besides, I was labeled as different by many people. I never liked to play ball or get sweaty. My favorite toy was Christmastime Barbie. When the boys used to roughhouse and try to do it to me, I'd tell them to leave me alone. I would never do anything that boys did, such as sports, play fighting, or singing to rap music.

I couldn't understand why the boys wanted to fight me when they didn't know a damn thing about me.

I could never understand why anyone would want to harass me for that. I used to think, "So what if I'm gay? So what if I'm different? Accept me or don't accept me at all, honey, because I'm just me." I couldn't understand why the boys wanted to bother me and fight me when they didn't know a damn thing about me. But they did.

The boys in my neighborhood were rough-necked, ball-playing, weed-smoking boys who picked on people to prove their machismo to their friends. I think those boys did what they did because of their own insecurities, because they wanted to prove they were manly men. There were about 9 or 10 of them and they lived in or around my neighborhood. Wherever I went I always ran into them, and often they would torture me for being gay.

One Halloween night, I went alone to catch the bus to go to a party. I was wearing a pair of dark jeans and a matching jacket and a black sweater with my initials on it. My mother had spent a lot for the outfit. The jacket alone cost $132.

While I was walking toward the bus, I saw a group of boys on bikes passing by. I recognized some of the guys. The first thought I had was, "Oh no, they're going to start trouble with me." I kept walking.

All of a sudden a partially opened bottle of urine hit me and got all over me. Some straight guys think doing something like that to a gay guy is kind of creative. They all hurried away and I screamed and cried because of all the money my mom spent on the outfit.

Then I felt the same as always—puzzled as to why I had to be their victim. I thought these guys would never understand me. They wanted to change me. They wanted to make me someone I wasn't. I felt like the things the boys said and did were marks for life.

For three weeks after Halloween, I had the incident on my mind. At first my brothers were trying to get me to let them beat the boys up. But I thought it would not make the situation better. It would probably just wild up the problem more.

Finally I decided that I'd show them I wouldn't stand for it anymore and I began to fight—with my pen. I wrote them gruesome letters smeared with ketchup for fake blood to let them know I was going to get them back and that I'd get the last laugh. Ha!

Usually, when the guys harassed me, I would tell them, "Go straight to hell because I'm going to be me and there will be no changes until I feel that my life needs a change." And I would get revenge. I would make fun of them trying to talk to girls and getting turned down. Then I would get physical with them because they tried to run my life, as if they were in my shoes living my life.

When we fought, often my brothers or my girl friends would be there to help me—some of my girl friends were known for beating guys down. And once I even whacked a guy with a plank. While I was fighting, I'd think blood and more blood, because of the traumatic experiences I'd been through. I wanted so much revenge on the boys who created trouble for me. Because of the fights, the cops were always at my house.

Even though it made me feel better for a short while to get revenge, I felt as if I was never going to succeed in having peace of mind. And after the fights were all over, I wouldn't feel much better. Often I felt as if I never belonged, and that no one would ever socialize with me because I was gay. I thought the world was so against me and that no one cared.

Still, there were people around who helped me and supported me, like my brothers and my friends. Looking back, I can see how much of a difference they made, even when times were at their hardest.

When I was living in my old neighborhood, my best friend was Lauryne. Beauty was her name, and we would go to the movies, the mall, or just hang in the park and talk about everything, from boys and love to clothes, shoes, and jewelry.

'Don't let no one turn you around,' my grandma told me.

Like a lot of my other girl friends, Lauryne didn't care that I was gay. As a matter of fact, she praised me for having the nerve to be able to come out at an early age to my parents and siblings and not really worry what they were going to think of me. She said things like, "You're brave," and that she was lucky to have a friend like me.

It made me feel wonderful to know I had friends who honestly cared about me. It made me strong and gave me courage to be even more open about my sexuality, and to encourage other kids to come into the light and take the risks. It made me believe there would always be people to support me.

Another person who really helped me survive everything was my grandma, who raised me. From my grandma I learned strength, courage, patience, love, heartfulness, and to treat all people the same no matter what. My grandma taught me to learn new things from people who try to reach out and teach you. She taught me the golden rule: Do unto others as you want others to do unto you.

My grandma was born in 1919. She grew up on a farm and was born in a time when blacks weren't accepted and women weren't allowed to vote. My grandma saw so much—the Great Depression, both World Wars, segregation, lynchings, civil rights. She would tell me about the marches, about the violence, and how once when she was in Jackson, Mississippi, she saw men cutting down two boys from a tree. She would tell me that life isn't that hard today, not after what she's seen and gone through. She told me, "My dear, you haven't seen the harshness life can give you."

Sometimes people who have lived through hard times grow closed and mean and bigoted against people who are different from them. But my grandma had a strong sense of herself, and that made her open-minded to the different things in life. She always said, "People must know themselves before they try to learn from another person," and that's exactly what she did.

As for my grandmother trying to change me, like so many other people in the world wanted to, it never happened. Instead, she encouraged me to do what I thought was right and what would make me happy. My grandma often told me I would be different as time went on and that she'd always love me however I was.

Three months after I came into foster care, when I was no longer living with my grandma because she was ill, I received a call from my aunt saying my grandma wanted to speak to me. When she got on the phone, she said, "I love you dear, and don't let no one turn you around." Then she hung up the phone because she had gotten short-winded. Shortly after that conversation, she died. I love her dearly and I miss her.

I now live in a group home for gay and transgendered boys. As for the boys in my neighborhood, they no longer bother me, because I don't go around there very often. When I think back on things, sometimes I can laugh, but other times I'm still angry that those nobodies had so much control over my life.

Still, I think I have come to be OK being myself every day. Despite all the hassles I went through, the people who supported

Rafael Manashirov

Standing My Ground

By Xavier Reyes

"Yo Xavier, are you down for smoking some buddha tonight?"

"Chill, not tonight, I'm too tired."

"Fine, b-tch."

"I'll be a b-tch, at least I don't survive on weed alone."

"Shut up."

"Yeah, whatever, just get out of my room."

"Yo, don't ever say #!?@ to me again!"

"Trust me, I won't!"

Everybody in my group home was going to smoke weed that night. I was the only one who refused, but I didn't say no because I was tired. I refused because I was being pressured into doing something that I was trying to break away from.

Each time the word "no" came from my mouth, I was losing friends. One by one they cursed me out and then left. But if my friends couldn't take no for an answer, then they weren't friends from the get-go.

Bullying was trying to take control of my life and I was fighting back. Every time I came face to face with it, I was determined to stand my ground.

Soon I had nobody to turn to in the group home but staff. I would talk to them about the things that I used to talk about with my friends, such as work, girls, sex, and drugs. We'd talk about these things and they'd give me advice on how to deal with them.

When my peers noticed I was talking with the staff, they started to call me "teacher's pet" and stuff like that. Even though I didn't show it, this hurt me deep inside. The staff knew what the other kids were saying, but told me to ignore them because they weren't heading anywhere in life except for the men's shelter.

It took a year for my peers to realize that they couldn't scare me into doing anything I didn't want to do.

The kids tried to turn everyone in the house against me. They would say things about me to the new kids in the home, and I wanted to mess them up. But I knew that was exactly what they wanted, so there was only one thing I could do: ignore them.

The other kids in the home began to steal things from me. They'd steal anything from personal hygiene stuff to underwear. One time the whole house ransacked my room. They stole bottles of cologne, clothes, jewelry, and more. The staff couldn't stop them, but they did help me get my stuff back.

After that incident, all the feelings that I had inside of me finally came to light—hatred, sadness, and anger. But I knew for a fact that I wasn't going to let these feelings take over my life and ruin it. No time soon was I about to give up. I was going to go out like a trooper, not like some damn wimp who couldn't control his feelings.

It took a year for my peers to realize that they couldn't scare me into doing anything I didn't want to do. After they finally learned this, things changed between us. They respected me for who I was, and I respected them for who they were.

Today there are still kids in the house who can't stand me but I don't care, because they aren't paying my bills or putting food in my stomach. So when they tell me they don't like me, I just tell them, "That's a personal problem," and walk away.

Nowadays things are much quieter for me in the group home. Once in a while the kids like to bother me, but it's only out of fun. The tension has eased up. Not everybody in the house is my friend, but I get along with everybody.

The main thing I learned out of this is to have confidence in myself and not to put myself down because of the things other people say or do to me. I don't have to follow other people just to be down, and if people can't respect my wishes and rights, then that's their problem, not mine.

By not giving into my peers, I gained self-esteem and self-respect. Bullying will always exist. Even though I seem to have defeated it, I know it isn't gone for good. It will continue to haunt me and you, and we have to keep fighting it.

Xavier was 16 when he wrote this story. He graduated from Baruch College in New York City, and later worked as an executive assistant at a major media company.

Nasty Girls

By Alice Wong

At the end of 8th grade, my classmates and I hung around after school signing each other's yearbooks. After my classmate Diana signed mine, I noticed she'd written, "Thank you for getting me into the gossip group."

I was shocked. I felt horrible. I didn't want people to associate me with a group labeled "the gossip group."

But the sad thing was, the girls in that gossipy group had been my closest friends for much of junior high. I don't know which I felt worse about—that I'd been part of their clique, or that they'd kicked me out of it.

I met the members of my clique—Maggie, Marsha, Kayla and Bethany—in 6th grade, the first year of junior high school. They were friendly and outgoing, and they helped me meet some new friends, too, which I liked since I was shy.

I was also naïve and thought everyone was kind. I thought my new friends were funny. They talked to me about their problems and I confided in them. They seemed to have all the qualities I was looking for in friends.

My new friends were also striving to be popular, and as the semester progressed, they got what they wanted. People in school knew who they were. For me, being part of a popular group was OK, but it wasn't as important as being accepted by a group.

But during that year, I also began to notice changes in their personalities. They seemed to think that being popular meant putting everyone else down.

Kayla was the leader of the group. People wouldn't know whether or not the rest of us agreed with what she said because we were robots; we went along with her even if our own opinions were different.

One day, Kayla pointed at an 8th grader in the hall and commented loudly on "what a big nose" he had. The group laughed, but I didn't. I thought it was rude.

I was afraid that if I spoke up, they'd all turn on me as well.

Another time, Kayla kept pointing at some guy and laughing. I didn't see anything funny about him, but the rest of the clique did. They noticed his crooked teeth. They tended to notice all the little imperfections about a person, things I didn't focus on when I saw someone.

They loved to label people "dorky" or "geeky." They gossiped about how people acted or what they'd heard about them through friends and acquaintances.

I often thought about what would happen if I told them how I felt when they were mean, but I was afraid to because I didn't want to lose their friendship. I was used to them and thought it would be too difficult to get to know a new group of people.

I was also afraid that if I spoke up, they'd all turn on me as well. I'd already had a taste of how it would feel to have their cruelty aimed at me.

One of the girls in the group, Bethany, had a particularly mean attitude and sometimes put me down like she did people outside our group. One day, I was wearing a Tommy Hilfiger shirt and she came over to check the label.

"Is that real?" she said in a very obnoxious and loud tone as she peered and tugged on the back of my shirt. Everyone just stared. My cheeks turned red from embarrassment.

She knew I wasn't the type who'd confront her, so she took advantage of my weakness. I felt hurt and angry that other members of the group did nothing to stick up for me. I was beginning to really dislike my friends. But I still wanted to be part of their group.

When 8th grade began, I hung with the clique during lunch and before and after school, but I also started to make new friends. I met people like Eva and Melissa in different classes. I could talk to them about things like our favorite bands and how we liked to sing and write poetry—things my old friends couldn't have cared less about.

Whenever I was with my new friends and saw the girls in my clique, it was awkward. I usually didn't introduce them to each other because I didn't think the girls in my clique would be interested in meeting my new friends.

Then one day, about three months before 8th grade ended, I sat down at my clique's usual lunch table. The clique was late, so I waited for them alone. After a few minutes, they came. Marsha and Maggie said, "Hi," but Bethany and Kayla said nothing.

I didn't know why they were acting so distant to me, but I thought if I just left it alone, they'd get over whatever was bothering them. So I went to where some of my other friends were sitting and chatted with them for a while.

When I came back to the clique's table, Kayla gave me this stare. I knew something was very wrong indeed. She said she had something to discuss with Marsha and didn't want me to listen to the conversation. I was like, "OK," but I felt left out.

I went to chat with my friend Jacqueline, who was sitting in the far corner of the lunchroom, but in the back of my mind I kept wondering what was up with the clique.

A few minutes later, the bell rang. On my way to the exit, Kayla called me over to the table. She told me that she didn't like that I associated with friends outside the clique. She said that if I wanted to remain in the group, I had to follow their rules. She didn't exactly say she wanted me out of the group, but it was obvious from her expression that she did.

I was beginning to really dislike my friends. But I still wanted to be part of their group.

The rest of the group just stared in silence at us; they already knew what she was going to say and do. Kayla snickered while she talked to me; she was having fun rejecting me.

I was shocked, and then, as her words sank in, it really started to hurt. For the rest of the day, I tried avoiding her. I felt like crying, but I didn't want to show her how badly her words hurt me.

When I got home, my mom saw how troubled I looked and asked, "What's wrong?"

"Not much. I just have a lot on my mind." I didn't feel like talking. I was very upset. But Mom was persistent. I finally spilled my guts.

She said things would get better. She assured me that everyone has problems like these, and I should accept that that's just how those girls were and that I couldn't change them; the only person I could change was myself.

But even though I'd known for a long time that they were mean to others, I couldn't accept that they'd been so cruel to me. I already missed them because I'd been a part of their group for so long.

For weeks, I didn't have much of a social life. I kept to myself during school. I didn't hang with anyone after school. I wasn't up to doing anything fun; I was too upset. All I wanted was to be alone and have time to think everything through.

I even lost my appetite. My mother prepared my favorite dishes, like barbecued spareribs and fried noodles, so that I'd eat, but I only ate small portions.

The way my friends turned on me made it hard to feel like I could trust anyone. I began analyzing everything anyone in the clique had said to me. I felt like I should've figured out how Kayla and Bethany were going to treat me before it was too late. I was scared that if I was open with my new friends, they'd wind up hurting me too.

But, noticing I was blue, my new friends e-mailed me jokes and poems to try to brighten my mood. At first, I was too upset to find the jokes funny. But after a few days, I reread their e-mails and they made me laugh.

One Saturday, Eva and Melissa dragged me out to the park to play basketball, twirl on the balance beams and ride our bikes. Then we went to McDonald's for lunch. I had so much fun. I began to realize who my true friends were.

Still, it wasn't until the end of the summer that I really started to feel better. Thankfully, making new friends wasn't that difficult after all.

I realized I should've left the old clique once I knew how they were instead of waiting until they forced me out. I'm glad I'm no longer part of that group. If I was, I might've become as closed-minded as they were and missed out on the opportunity to meet new people.

I still feel guilty for the years I was a friend to those girls. Even though I didn't do most of the mean things they did, I continued to be a part of their group.

I'm still cool with the other friends I made in 8th grade. And when I went to high school, I was relieved to find that most people were much more respectful toward each other than in my junior high. I started associating with all sorts of people who were friendly and kind. I didn't care anymore if I fit into any one group.

Now I realize that being in a clique doesn't determine my worth. When I was in the clique, people in and out of the group saw me as naïve, and I was closed-minded to new people. Now people see me as an outgoing, friendly and kind person, which is a more accurate reflection of who I am and want to be.

Alice was 17 when she wrote this story. She has since graduated from Baruch College in New York City, where she majored in journalism.

David Najarro

Caught Between Two Colors

By Shaniqua Sockwell

When I was a little girl growing up in the Bronx, I would sit on the front steps of my apartment building and watch people walk by. White people, Spanish people, Indian people, and of course, black people. A world full of color, each person unique and special in her own way.

And I began to wonder: Why, with all this beauty in the world, must we hurt one another? Why can't we love our differences, rather than hate each other for them?

Which brings me to the subject of my story. If anyone knows anything about being hated for being different, it's me.

From the time I was 3, I was always told by friends, teachers, and even family that I was "different" from "everyone else." They didn't tell me exactly how I was different or who "everyone else" was, but when I was 7 years old I found out.

There was a girl at school named Maxine who would pick fights with me every day and do her best to get me yelled at. Whenever she got herself in trouble, she would find a way to blame me. I seemed to be the only person she ever picked on and she made my life miserable. She was, in a sense, my own personal bully.

One day after school, Maxine and her friends caught up with me while I was walking home. She tapped me on the shoulder and said, "Hey Shaniqua, what you get on the history test?"

"I got an 80. Why?" I asked.

She pinned me against a car and yelled, "Well, I only got a 65, b-tch! You should've let me see your test paper, but you had to be Ms. Goody Two-Shoes, didn't you?"

"Let go of me! At least you passed!" I said.

She pulled back her hand like she was ready to slap me, but instead she turned to her friends and said, "You ain't even worth it." Then she shoved me. "Bye, you wanna-be white b-tch!"

I don't know why, but when she said that, something inside me clicked. As Maxine was walking away I said, "I'm not a wan-na-be white b." (I was never comfortable cursing.)

She turned back around and started to laugh. Then she said, "Who you think you foolin'? You walk white, talk white, and you dress white, too. With all that preachin' you be doing at school about love and understandin', I thought at least you'd act like your own people. But no, you gotta be Ms. Proper."

"Don't nobody in school talk like you 'cept the white kids," Maxine said.

Maxine snickered. I glared at her and said, "I never said I was proper and I don't go around preaching anything."

"Do you listen to yourself?" she asked me. Her friends said they had to go, which left me alone with Maxine.

"Listen to you. Don't nobody in school talk like you 'cept the white kids. Instead of sayin', 'Yeah,' you say, 'Yes.' Instead of sayin', '#!?@ you,' you say, 'Forget you.' I don't know if you know it or not, but you is different with a capital D! If you ain't realized that yet, you's one blind b-tch!"

I didn't want to say that I'd been hearing I was different for a long time now (especially since the way Maxine said it made me think it was really true).

So instead I said, "Oh, so you're saying that I've got to dress in tight clothes, get bad grades, and talk with broken English in order to be normal."

"B-tch, I ain't sayin' #!?@ 'cept this. Before you start talkin' about black this and black that, find the black in you first. Bye b-tch, see ya tomorrow." Then she walked away.

So that's what everyone meant when they said I was "different." They thought I acted white and not black. "Is that a bad thing?" I wondered.

I thought about what Maxine said as I walked the rest of the way home, and I tried to convince myself that I was black. I kept on repeating to myself, "I am black, I am black." Wasn't I?

When I finally got home my brothers were watching TV, but when they saw me they jumped up and said, "Nica, we hungry."

I went over and gave them a kiss and said, "Daddy never came over to make dinner for you?"

"He in kitchen," Lewis said. "But he cook too slow."

"What about Mommy?" I said.

"She no come home," Lewis said. He had this sad, faraway look in his eyes. I hugged him and told him everything was going to be alright, although I wasn't so sure myself. I knew why she wasn't home, and, even though they were young, so did my brothers.

She was out getting high and it was no secret to us. I wish she knew what kind of pain she was putting us through. Maybe if she did know, she wouldn't have been out there shooting up and sniffing her life away.

I went in the kitchen and saw my father searching in the fridge. When he finally looked up and saw me, he said, "Hey girl, what's up."

"Nothing much," I said. "Could I talk to you for a sec?"

"Sure, honey. Just a sec." He looked in the fridge and sucked his teeth. "Looks like you'll be going to Grandma's house tonight to eat." Then he closed it. "OK, what's up?"

"Well, there's this girl named Maxine in my school and she told me that I act white. People say that I act different, and I think that's what they mean. Do you think there's something wrong with me?"

"Sweetie, come here."

I sat down in the chair in front of him.

"Now, there's nothing wrong with you. You're a smart young lady for your age. There is nothing wrong with the way you act. Just because you don't talk or walk like everyone else, that's no reason to feel uptight about yourself. There is no one way to be, anyway. So if someone teases you about something, don't listen to them. Just believe in yourself."

"Thanks Daddy," I said, and hugged him.

After my little talk with Dad, I was no longer afraid to express myself, whether I "sounded white" (whatever that means) or not. I got over my fear of being "different" by believing in myself.

From that point on I avoided Maxine. Whenever she tried to start trouble with me, I would tell her to leave me alone.

If someone like Maxine ever happens to come along and harass you because they find you different, just tell her: "You can harass me if you want to and call me names, but no matter what you do, I'm gonna be who I am."

My message is this: Whether you are white and "act black" or are black and "act white," we all bleed, cry, laugh, and die the same way. It doesn't matter what people say about you or what's on the outside. It's what's on the inside and what you think about yourself that counts.

Shaniqua was 16 when she wrote this story.

Elizbeth Deegan

Sticks and Stones

By Yen Yam

I always thought being Chinese was a curse. When I was growing up, I lived in a mostly black neighborhood. I had friends but I didn't fit in. At first, I didn't think too much about my race. Then, in 1st grade, two boys started calling me "small eyes" and making kung fu noises. I didn't know what it meant; I was only 6 years old.

Much later, when I was watching a Bruce Lee movie and saw him making the same stupid noises, I finally realized that they were messing with me because I am Asian. Their jokes were only the beginning. Growing up, I was constantly made fun of because of my name, my looks, the way I talk, everything

Even my friends teased me. One girl would always say, "Yenny Yam, how about some egg rolls," and another friend would say, "Chin chun chun," and then squint his eyes at me.

I know that sometimes they were only joking around, but it really hurt my feelings, even though I never said anything about it. I don't think my friends thought it was hurtful, but they knew it was embarrassing for me because my face would become red and they would laugh about it.

Most of my friends were black, and some never said anything racist to me and would defend me to others. But their help was not enough.

And the teasing wasn't the worst of it. One very clear and sunny day, my cousin Amy and I were taking the long way home from school, walking through the parking lot of a Baptist church. We saw two kids we knew from school, Damien and Shawn.

They yelled crude remarks at us, like, "Chin chun, egg rolls, Chun Lee," and some other mean words regarding our race. Amy yelled at them to shut up and go away. That was when they started to throw rocks at us. One rock hit me straight in the chest. It hurt so much and I got a huge bruise.

I didn't tell anyone because I was a quiet and shy girl and I was always too scared to say anything. I think that made me an even bigger target. But Amy did tell her brother, and he went to talk to Damien's mother.

I was most angry at my black peers, because it seemed like they should have known better.

The next day, Shawn told me that he had a huge sister and she was going to beat me up if I got his friend in trouble again. I was scared. After that, I began to think that I was not a kid anymore. People would hurt me if I said something they didn't like.

I was not just teased by black people, but by white and Hispanic people, too. When I was 8, two white boys would throw rocks and sticks at us and call us names. But, often, I was most angry at my black peers, because it seemed like they should have known better.

I am not writing this to disrespect African-Americans. But I would wonder why black kids were making racist remarks to me when they should have known better than anyone that it is not right. They should have thought of what their ancestors had been through—and their parents and grandparents, and themselves—and realized that they were doing the same thing.

When teachers would teach us about slavery, civil rights, and segregation in class, the black students would talk about how they are treated unfairly because of their skin color.

I used to sit in class and think that they were talking a lot of junk. They would mess with me one minute and the next they would make an about-face. They would say crude things to my face, then preach that it is wrong to judge by skin color.

I don't think they realized they were being hypocritical. When people think "racism," they tend to think "black and white." But the way the people in my school acted toward me was racist, and getting treated like I was not even worth the dirt they stood on really hurt me. It made me angry. It also made me feel ashamed of being Asian.

I have never been sure whether to fight back or stay silent. I am afraid if I do say something back, it will just make people even more cruel.

One time I did speak my mind, and it only made things worse. I was working in my family's restaurant when a couple of guys started to say some perverted stuff about Asian girls. I got mad and started to argue with one guy. He ended up grabbing a container full of rice that we use as a paperweight and throwing it at my head. I ducked and it missed my head by inches.

I was scared, but I looked him in the eye, staring him down, trying to make it seem like I wasn't afraid of him. Inside, I wanted to cry.

I think I'm too small to fight back, but I wish I could. I think people tend to believe Asians are a weak race and are not able to stand up for ourselves, so it makes me feel weak when I make that stereotype seem true.

But at least my brother Prince always stands up for himself. Once, when he and his friend were eating pizza, two teens started to call them names, wanting to start a fight. They were surprised when he and his friend fought back. I am not a person who likes violence, but I was proud that my brother fought them, even if he did sprain his wrist.

Even worse than feeling angry is feeling ashamed of who I am. When I was younger, I used to wish I was a white girl with a white girl's name. I loved their big, light eyes and light hair colors. Instead, I had plain, dark brown hair and small, dark brown eyes.

Even worse than feeling angry is feeling ashamed of who I am.

When I used to play house or hotel or school with my cousin, we would always become white and I would pretend my name was Elizabeth White. I also pretended that I was rich, because back then I thought all white people were rich.

I used to wish that I was able to change my name for real, because no one else had such a weird name—Yen Yam. I used to hate having my name called out because someone would always have a comment about it. It wasn't until I moved to New York and started high school that I met many people with unusual names. Before, I felt like I was standing out like a sore thumb.

You might think with all these angry feelings that I would become bitter and hateful toward others. But I don't treat people differently because of their skin color. I'm a shy girl, and I get to know people before I have an opinion about them.

Besides, I've always known people who don't judge by skin color. I want to be like those people, not like the people who have hurt me.

I know racism really comes from ignorance. I even see that in my own family. When I was growing up they would sometimes say that black people are dirty or bad people. I would always say that there are dirty and bad Chinese people, too. But it is hard to change old ways of thinking.

I think the way the older people in my family grew up has a

lot to do with why they look down on other races. They grew up in China, where they knew only Chinese people. In the United States, they are unable to communicate with others. So they just think the worst, based on what they hear from their friends.

The people who were messing with me were similar, in a way, because they didn't know anything about Chinese people. They based their comments on what they had seen on TV.

Right now, I don't know how I should feel, though. Should I still feel angry at the people who have done this to me? Should I get revenge? Should I feel sad? I don't know. I'm confused about everything.

At least I don't feel like my heritage is a curse anymore. Over time, I've become more comfortable with who I am. But sometimes I still feel lost and alone. Sometimes I wonder, "Where do I belong?"

I was born in the United States and don't speak much Chinese. So here I am different because of my skin color. In China, I would be regarded as an idiot, an outsider, because I do not understand the language.

Sometimes I feel like an alien who doesn't fit anywhere in this world. It's strange to belong to no country and to feel like you have no people of your own.

Yen was 18 and in high school when she wrote this story.

Allajah Young

'Can I Holla Atcha?'

By Allajah Young

It's a hot, humid July day on Manhattan's Upper West Side, too hot to sit in the house. So my younger sister Ni and I venture out for ices.

The trip across the street to the ices cart isn't long, so I leave on my white tank top and put on a knee-length denim skirt and flip-flops. Too busy trying to decide whether I want cherry or mango, I fail to notice him leaning against a building next to the cart.

"Damn, Ma," he says.

What's that supposed to mean? Is that supposed to be a compliment? I instantly become unfriendly. He has the audacity to think I'm so simple. I roll my eyes as my face becomes rigid and mean.

"That boy's calling you, Allajah," says Ni, so innocently.

"Why does he have to say something?" I grunt to myself.

"Why you look so mean?" he says from under his oversized Yankees cap, which sits so low that I almost can't tell he's staring at me.

"Do you know him from your school?" Ni asks, puzzled.

"You know why I look so mean? Because I don't like you," I say to myself.

It's like I'm a car crash on the side of the highway, with men slowly rubbernecking their way past me.

I am so weary of the idea that catcalls are an appropriate way to approach a girl on the street.

Catcalls can be tame, like "Pssss, pssss, where you live?" or outright dirty, like "Can you let me hit that?" It can be from one wanna-be-a-player guy on 125th Street in Harlem or from a group of delusional school-boys on wealthy Madison Avenue.

Sometimes I can see it coming. I can see him looking at me lecherously from halfway down the block and no matter how much I look away, he can't hold back the comment that rolls off his tongue into my face.

"Damn, can I carry your bag?"

Or a dirty, raspy, "Hey sexy thang!"

And the common, "Can I holla atcha?"

But sometimes they come out of left field and take me by surprise, like the police officer who says, "God bless you, girl," as I pass him by. Street harassment's becoming more and more a part of my daily life. And the older I get, the more it exasperates me.

Am I supposed to turn around and smile at you, delighted by your observation? Who are you looking for? The girl who turns around. The one whose standards aren't too high. The one who's sure to give you her number and go to your house the next day.

Those comments may work with those women, but not with me. I feel uncomfortable when I'm gawked at or commented on. It's degrading. It's like I'm a car crash on the side of the highway, with men slowly rubbernecking their way past me so they can survey my every detail. I simply don't respond, hoping they won't keep bothering me if I ignore them.

My boyfriend attributes the catcalls to the way most of my pants fit. Not that my pants are skin tight, but they are close. Still, even if my pants were painted on, does this give the dirty man in the corner store permission to stare directly at my behind as if I was the last piece of cake on the dessert cart?

Or if my top is cut low, does this give my teacher permission to stare directly down my shirt like he dropped something down there? Just like it's impolite to stare at the homeless or disabled, men shouldn't stare at a woman as if she's a movie poster.

Some men blame women for their harassment by saying that we dress provocatively and therefore want the stares and crass comments. But that argument has no merit, because unless a women is walking down the street naked and screaming, "Come sleep with me!" what she wears is not necessarily an indication of what she wants sexually. Women wear tight pants and little shirts because we like them and they're commonly in stores.

And sometimes women try to outdress each other by wearing sexy outfits. A woman may want to be a sharp dresser in order to feel better about herself and feel attractive, not because she wants to be harassed by men.

Besides, we're still bothered even when we're not attractively dressed. When it's -2 degrees outside and I have on a pair of extra large sweat pants, a huge bubble coat, and a fleece hat and scarf wrapped so tight on my head that only my eyes show, some simpleton will still say, "Yo. What up! Can I talk to you for a minute?"

I'm 17 and already feel like the harassment never ends. So I'm troubled when I see younger girls being harassed. I worry about Ni, who's only 11, and other girls her age because they're most susceptible to catcalls. They're often too young to see the lust and disrespect behind the comments and stares.

I think some leftover animal instinct makes men stare, but

that's no excuse for having no self-control. It's all right to glance at a woman you're attracted to, but to stare her down is unnecessary.

It's unfortunate that some girls and women welcome catcalls. This makes it harder for those of us with a certain level of self-respect. When I ignore the catcall games, I'm looked at like I'm the crazy one. But this doesn't faze me much because I don't want to be friends with someone who harasses women.

Sadly, I don't think I could stop the daily annoyances unless I shave my head or dress like a boy. But why should I have to? I'm not asking for much, just a little consideration.

So guys, if you're attracted to a girl you see on the street, approach her respectfully. Instead of jumping out from an alley and saying, "Yo pants is tiiiiiigggggggghhhhhhht!!" try to approach her when she's waiting to cross the street.

Say, "Hello, how are you doing?" or "Excuse me, can I have a word with you?" Try to be calm and civilized. Remember, a vulgar comment will often completely reverse your chances of actually talking with the girl you're interested in.

Think about how you'd feel if the tables were turned and you had to deal with street harassment. I'm sure if, every day, you had to hear a big-bodied woman loudly proclaim to you how she wants to "hit that ass," you wouldn't be so quick to tell me the same. If you lived with that on a daily basis, you'd see why street harassment's so wearisome for women to cope with.

Allajah was 17 when she wrote this story.

Chris Pope

Karate Killed the Monster Inside Me

By Robin Chan

I was fed up. From the time I was 4 years old, I was teased and pushed around by bullies on my way home from school because I was short and frail-looking. My family and I also got harassed by racist punks because we were the only Asian people living in a white neighborhood.

These incidents grew the hate monster inside of me. Most days, I would come home from elementary school either angry or crying. My family and friends tried to comfort me, but I had been storing up the loads of anger inside me for too long. I thought I was going to explode.

When I was about 9, I found the answer to my problems. I decided to learn karate so I could break the faces of all the people on my "hit list" (anyone who had ever bullied me or my family).

I started nagging my parents about learning karate. They agreed because they wanted me to build up my self-esteem, learn some discipline, and have more self-confidence. All I wanted was to learn the quickest way to break someone's neck, but I didn't tell that to my parents.

I was about 10 years old when I finally got my chance. My first dojo (that's what martial arts students call the place where they study and practice) was small, musky, and smelled lightly of sweat. The instructor, Mr. Sloan, was as strict as an army drill sergeant.

I decided to learn karate so I could break the faces of all the people on my 'hit list.'

Mr. Sloan taught us how to do strange abdominal exercises that were like upside down sit-ups and really difficult to do. He wouldn't allow any slacking off from people who got tired. It was only the first day, what did he want from us? I quickly discovered that I was really out of shape. Before the first lesson was over, I was already thinking about dropping out.

By the end of the second lesson, however, I had decided to stick with it. Mr. Sloan was teaching us cool techniques for breaking out of arm and wrist locks and that got me interested.

Mr. Sloan was a good instructor. Within a few months, my class of beginners went from learning the basic punch, block, and kick, to learning a flying jump kick. He also taught us effective techniques for breaking out of headlocks and strangleholds. We enhanced our skills by sparring with each other and practicing at home.

Although the dojo had limited resources (there were no boards to break, no martial arts weapons, and no fighting gear), I still learned a lot and had a lot of fun. I became more flexible from the rigorous exercises. In addition to practicing our karate moves, we did push-ups, sit-ups, and leg, arm, torso, and back stretches to limber up.

We also meditated together. Near the end of class, Mr. Sloan would "guide" us through the meditation by telling us to clear our minds. One time, he told us to picture ourselves breaking free of a barrier or knocking a barrel or a wall to pieces. He said that whenever we had problems or faced challenges that got us frustrated, we should go to a quiet place, relax, and close our eyes. In our minds, we should picture ourselves knocking over that problem or challenge. Mr. Sloan said that doing this should make us feel better. After meditating on "killing" the problem, he said, our minds would be clear and we'd be more determined to solve it.

Mr. Sloan also made it clear that he was teaching us karate not just so we'd be able to kick someone's ass real good, but so each of us could become a role model. A role model, he explained, was someone with a good conscience, good morals, self-respect, and respect for others.

We worked on developing these qualities in class by bowing to the instructor, addressing him as "sir" or "sensai," treating fellow students with respect, and listening to our sensai's lectures, which taught us about respect, discipline, manners, and so on. We were taught to exercise these qualities not only in the dojo, but outside as well.

The goal of becoming a role model was a major factor in my wanting to continue to study karate. I no longer saw the martial arts as a way to get back at people who hurt me. I knew from experience that there were enough menacing and evil people in this world. I didn't want to become one of them.

After a few months, I was much more self-confident and disciplined. I knew that I was now capable of protecting myself against enemies. Whether or not I chose to fight someone who bullied me was beside the point; I knew that I could knock them out. Just knowing that made me feel good about myself, so why fight when you're already ahead? Besides, not fighting would save my knuckles from a lot of pain.

The insults and slurs I encountered did not bother me as much anymore. As a matter of fact, the discipline and basic philosophy I learned from karate held back the punches I was tempted to throw when people tried to provoke me to fight.

For example, one day when I was walking home from school, two teenaged guys walked into me. One of them said, "Watch it, ch-nk" and shoved me. They started pushing me but I just blocked their pathetic pushes. They weren't getting enough thrills from just shoving me, so they started cursing and spitting at me too.

The discipline and basic philosophy I learned from karate held back the punches I was tempted to throw

I started getting really aggravated. Then I remembered something Mr. Sloan had told me when I asked him what to do when someone bothers you. "Low-lifes like these do not deserve the time and energy you put into punching them out," he said. "Just walk away and splash some cold water on your face."

I cooled down and started walking away. The two guys saw that I was not affected by their stupid remarks. I heard one of them say, "Forget that ch-nk, man."

It was ironic how I wanted to learn karate so that I could beat up people like these, and then, when I got the chance, I didn't go through with it. What karate taught me was that fighting isn't the right way to solve a problem. It just turns you into one of those low-lifes who don't have the conscience, respect, manners, or education to know how to handle their problems any other way.

I was good enough at karate by that point that it wouldn't have been a fair fight. But if I had given in to the temptation to beat those guys up, I would have felt ashamed and guilty. I would have disappointed Mr. Sloan, who taught me that the most important rule of karate is not to fight unless it's necessary for self-defense; my parents, who told me never to fight with anyone even if they are wrong; and myself, because I feel that it is wrong to take advantage of a situation.

The time and effort I was putting into karate was getting me worthwhile results. I used to be wild when I was with my friends, but I had become more reserved and well-behaved. I also used to slack off in school but not anymore. I really started gearing up and hitting the books. My teachers and parents noticed the difference and were happy with what they saw.

I was even becoming a role model for some of my friends. They told me that they had never seen me work so hard before, and they admired the high grades I was earning in school. They decided to follow my example and started pulling their acts together and improving their own grades.

Unfortunately, Mr. Sloan's class ran for only a year and when time was up, all of us were really upset. But our instructor had a new class of misfits to turn into the fine role models we had become.

Studying karate was a wonderful experience. I'm thankful to my extraordinary and deserving instructor, Mr. Sloan, and to my great family who let me go to the dojo and have supported me always. Together, Mr. Sloan and my parents have made me realize that I should always try my best and put a sincere effort into whatever I do. They have geared me up, morally and spiritually, to reach for the stars.

The author was 16 when he wrote this story. After college and graduate school, he became a flight surgeon for the U.S. Air Force.

Karolina Zaniesienko

Bad Boy Gets a Conscience

By Anonymous

From the age of 10 to age 14, I was a monster. It was as if my conscience had taken a long vacation. I did horrible things to people
and didn't care.

I ripped into other kids and mocked them till they cried. My
friends and I called one kid "Bobby the Beaver" because of his
teeth. We gnawed on pencils in front of him, making him squirm.
And the other kids would laugh. We thought we were funny.

At school, I went into people's desks or bags and took their
snacks or CDs. I stole from stores for the fun of it, too. I did it
once and I got away with it, so that inspired me to do it again.

I enjoyed going into nice neighborhoods, like the Upper East
Side of Manhattan, and scratching up expensive cars. I'd find a
big gaudy car, like a Benz or a Lexus. Then I'd wait until no one
was looking and scratch my initials on the trunk, and put "album

coming soon."

I never stopped to think why I did these things. I did them because I could.

But now, a lot of people see me as Mr. Rogers, because I'm mostly friendly and unassuming. I do well in school. I'm helpful and polite. Most people assume that I've always been a good guy, but that's far from the case.

I think I got so mean because when I was younger, people in school picked on me. I had a bit of a stammer, and I was taller than most of the class. I was a very hyper but nice kid, but I got the vibe that people didn't like me and thought of me as stupid. We played charades once in class and though the correct word was "stupid," several kids called out my name as the answer. That hurt.

I had one close friend, but he left in 4th grade, and then I didn't have any friends. The other kids in school avoided me and the girls ran away from me in the yard. I felt alienated.

Since people didn't like me, I thought I might as well give them a reason. I started chasing the girls around and making monster noises. They hated it. But I thought it was funny.

Being picked on made me angry, and I started to fight back.

I turned being bigger to my advantage. My favorite activity was sitting on people. If someone said or did something to me, I'd push him on the floor and sit on him. "I could do this all day," I'd say. "I'm not getting off you until you apologize to me." I got my apologies.

I wanted respect, and I discovered that if I was tough, people respected me. Or maybe they feared me—I didn't understand the difference. I fought over anything. I'd take on kids younger than me, my age, or older, whole groups, girls—anybody, as long as I thought I could win.

I liked the power I commanded over the situation and that made my actions bolder over time. I took things up a notch. A stare deserved a smart-ass comment, a smart-ass comment deserved a push, a push deserved a few punches, a few punches deserved getting stomped.

When I got to junior high school I was able to use my "talents" to acquire a group of like-minded friends. I was in charge. I admired my friends' humor, though. I'd point someone out and they would start dissing them.

I was particularly horrible to a kid named Billy. One time, I'd gotten a buzz-cut and he goofed on me. That annoyed me, so he became my pet project. For 10 months I did nothing but insult him. I'd get everybody to laugh at him in class or in the lunchroom. When we learned we were getting a snow day, I pointed to Billy and told him, "We'll get two days off if you stand on the roof and shake your head," because of his dandruff.

I enjoyed being able to hurt people with words. We even harassed the teachers. One teacher quit after his first few months with us, and we went through five more until the school found someone who could keep us more in check.

There was one teacher, though, who I respected. He was laid back and friendly, and he treated me like I could think and understand. He thought I was a smart kid and I took that to heart. He lent me a book about rap history and taught me to play chess.

And then there was Lisa. She was different from the other girls at my school. She was into art, books, classical music, and school—everything I wasn't. She was the first girl I fell in love with.

I think I was attracted to her because she acted so different and I wanted to know why. In my last year of junior high, I asked her to tutor me in math because it was the easiest way to start talking to her.

I acted really nice toward Lisa and we talked a lot during our tutoring sessions. Our conversations brought out my intellectual side. I was able to take the things I learned through my teacher and apply them to the conversations with Lisa. She expected me to understand things and that made me feel good. I came to really love her and enjoy her company.

But when Lisa caught on to how I felt for her, she totally crushed me. She sat me down one day and said, "I know that you like me."

"How did you know?" I asked.

She said she'd been reading Seventeen and there was a quiz, "Does one of your friends like you?"

"I took the test and it described you," she said. Then she said she could never see herself with me. "I think you're a horrible person," she said. "Get away from me."

It surprised me, because she was the first person I was ever really good to and I thought she at least liked me as a person. I was kind of numb for a while, and then I was in pain.

She stopped tutoring me and we stopped talking. And whenever her friends were around, she'd make a negative comment about me loud enough for me to hear it.

I never let anything faze me, but that did. I couldn't say anything back because I cared about her too much to hurt her. I felt the way I must've made people feel, small and hurt.

Around the same time, I had another experience that threw me off course. My friends and I were hanging out with some girls from

I didn't know how to act toward people if they weren't in fear of me.

school, and one girl was hanging on my friend Tommy. Suddenly, some high school guys ran up. They were a lot bigger than we were. The girl with Tommy was seeing one of them, and he walked up to Tommy, punched him and pushed him on the ground.

I ran. I left out of fear. I picked fights I could win, and I didn't think I could win this one. Some of my friends were mad at me. They questioned my loyalty. But I hated to lose a fight.

One of my friends really took it to heart and trashed me in school the next day. "You ran out on Tommy," he yelled at me.

"Well, you ran out, too," I shot back.

"I left to call the police. Where did you go?" he said.

We almost came to blows in front of everybody in the auditorium, but a teacher broke us up. The incident polarized my group of friends. While some supported me, I stopped hanging out with most of them.

These combined dramas took all the joy out of my work of being nasty. I got really depressed in the last couple of weeks of junior high school. I felt heartbroken by Lisa and bummed by what happened between my friends.

My friends ended up going to a different high school from me, which only increased our distance. And when I started high school, I didn't know anyone. I got really reclusive and I sank into a depression. I didn't have my heart in harming people anymore. I tried it a few times, just to get my confidence going, but it didn't work.

I started having nightmares where I'd be fighting what seemed like a marathon of people, until I couldn't fight anymore and was destroyed by the constant swarm of people coming at me. Looking back, it was fitting punishment for the way I'd treated people.

In junior high I had so much power, but in high school I was nothing. I was anonymous and, more than anything, that drove me crazy. I wanted the same attention I got before, but I didn't want to harm people anymore. I didn't have guilt yet over what I did; I just didn't have the same sense of fun I used to have when I did something mean-spirited.

Without friends, I had nothing to do after school, so I'd read and write to pass the time. And because I was reading so much on my own, I started doing well in school. I could understand schoolwork much quicker than I had before.

But I had no meaningful contact with anyone for two years. I felt that I didn't know how to act toward people if they weren't in fear of me. I'd had few relationships that didn't revolve around my control of people. I became very brooding and quiet.

The closest I came to interacting with people was when I

worked on the school newspaper, as editor. Most of the time I left comments on the writers' articles, rather than talk to them in person. Usually, after school or on weekends, I'd go to a bookstore or a library, or I'd go to the movies by myself.

But I became sick of feeling anonymous. I wanted a change. The first thing I did was change schools. I applied and got into an alternative school in the city.

My goal when I left my old high school was to learn how to be social and to interact normally with people my own age. I had to learn how to communicate my feelings and ideas without being mean or aggressive. I also had to learn to respect people and not to insist on what I wanted.

I felt that by trying to help people, I could make up for my past of harming people.

First, I started observing people. When I used to pick on people, I'd study them to see where they might be vulnerable. So I thought I should also study people I wanted to be my friends.

I'd watch people and the way they interacted. I made mental notes, like, "This girl touches her friends as she talks to them; she's outgoing and seems well-liked."

Then, I tried striking up conversations on the subway or bus, and in school. Sometimes people would open up to me during these encounters, and I began to see people in a whole new light.

I began to see the beauty of people, something that never really struck me till I started to interact with them. I saw how frail a person can be, or honest, or compassionate, or smart, or funny. I developed a sense of empathy. I started to understand what people are going through and have been through to act the way they do.

One person who helped set me on my current path was Anna. I met her on the bus. It was the first time I'd ever talked to a girl outside of school.

She had headphones on and I could hear the music, so I

decided to ask her about it. I was nervous because she was beautiful, and my experience of interacting with pretty girls was that they usually looked down on me. When I introduced myself to her, I said my full name and she said, smiling, "I am Anna and the rest of my name I can't pronounce." She was funny and had a sarcasm that made her approachable.

I told her I was 16, and she said, "Aww, you're a baby." (She was 20, but looked younger.) If someone had said something like that to me before, I would've gotten upset, but the way she said it sounded like a compliment.

Anna was from Europe and would fall into an accent when she told stories about life in her country. We didn't spend much time together, but we'd talk on the phone once or twice a week. Then, for a week, I tried calling and couldn't reach her.

When I did, she sounded sad. She told me her best friend had died and she was too depressed to do anything. It bothered me hearing her upset. But during our talk, I was able to make her laugh a few times and she told me that was the first time she'd laughed since her friend's death.

Making her feel better made me feel good. I was happy I could do that for her. Even though she moved away soon after that and we lost touch, my friendship with Anna made me realize how good it felt to help someone.

I got excited by my new concern. I liked learning about new people and trying to figure them out. I also felt that by trying to help people, I could make up for my past of harming people and being so indifferent to them.

I mainly talked to girls because they're generally more open to conversation. I was able to learn a lot about people because if I asked a girl what she was thinking or feeling, she'd usually tell me. Most guys would just say, "Nothing." But my best friend now is a guy, Otis, whom I knew in my depressed stage. We developed a relationship as I built more confidence.

Now I enjoy connecting with people and I learn a lot about myself as I observe others. One day I decided to talk to Shelly, a girl in my class, because it seemed that no one else was paying attention to her. I thought she was smart, but she later told me that people talked down to her. I knew what that felt like.

She reminded me of myself. I know what it's like to be alone and I don't like thinking that other people are alone. Most people have their issues, but they're good at heart.

With Shelly, there's a high level of trust—I can tell her things and be vulnerable to her in the way that she can be vulnerable to me. She helps me feel better about things, too.

I don't expect a reward for how I've changed. Over time, I've learned that my goal shouldn't be to redeem myself, as if "poof!" what I did in the past can be erased. What makes me happy is relating to people, having them trust me, and letting them know that they're not all alone.

The author was in high school when he wrote this story.

John Gaston

Releasing My Rage

By Miguel Ayala

I've had an anger problem for a long time. It has included crying, yelling, cursing, screaming, and intimidating people. When I was at my worst, I would turn violent and destroy property and throw things. I even tried to kill myself.

The reason I have an anger problem is plain and simple. I grew up in a violent home. My mother would slap, whip, and beat me and my siblings. Also, she would torment us with words that to this day still hurt me. She would call us terrible names if one of us dyed our hair or for messing up on paperwork she was supposed to do. She would beat us for the smallest things, like making noise, or playing too rough in the house, or accidentally breaking things. She'd beat us until we bled or had welts all over our bodies.

That wasn't the only side of her. Sometimes she would laugh

with us, take us on family outings, nurture us, and really show a mother's love. Those times, I really loved her. All this love and hate mixed together made me very confused and angry. Sometimes I took the anger out on myself, other times on other people.

When I was 12 my mother gave me $7.50 for a class trip, and instead I bought a video game magazine. She found out and whipped me with an extension cord.

That night I felt so much anger, I didn't know what to do with it. So I contemplated two horrible things. I thought of sneaking out of the apartment, going to my roof, saying a prayer, and then jumping off. And I contemplated hurting my mother. I imagined getting a knife, tip-toeing into my mother's bedroom, and killing her.

In the end, I made it through that night without hurting myself or her. But the worst of my anger was yet to come.

Back then, I never released my rage on my mother. I was afraid that if I did, she might kill me or beat me to the point where I'd be disabled. So instead, I took my rage out on other people, usually at school. I would fight and steal. Many times I would curse at people in public and say obscene things to females. I was a terrible bully.

It made me feel a little better to do those things. It made me feel like I had all the guts in the world, and it released my rage *It released my rage to make other people as mad as I felt.* to make other people as mad as I felt. The only problem was that those people would always want to whip my butt for it. Sometimes they did.

Then one day I really lost it. It was a beautiful, warm day. I was 14 or 15. I lost a music cassette tape. At first that didn't bother me. Then I started imagining that my mother and brother had taken it just to see me get mad. Thinking this made me angry. I started yelling at my brother and my mom. Then I really went crazy. I was crying, and before I knew it, I'd gone to the china cabinet in the kitchen and rammed my elbow into the glass cover. I cut myself pretty bad. That's when my family sent me to the hospital.

The doctor who bandaged my cut asked me a bunch of questions to see why I did it. But I brushed them off, and said I just lost my temper. They thought of sending me to a residential treatment center where I could get help with my anger, but my mother wouldn't sign the papers to let me go. Looking back, it might have been a good thing for me to go to a residential treatment center where I would have been away from home and might have gotten a lot of adult attention and more mental health services. Instead, I kept living with abuse and feeling angry.

I did go to a school in a hospital because of my behavior problems. There I had therapy and group meetings three times a week for almost two years. They were trying to get me to work on my problems: Fights, Acting Out, Acting on Impulse, and, my personal favorite, Self-Destructive Behaviors, like when I tried to sharpen my finger in a metal pencil sharpener.

The school was good for me because it gave me a support network of adults who cared. I had all these people who wanted to help me with my problems. It felt like winning the lottery.

Eventually I began to open up to those people. I told one of them that I was contemplating suicide. Telling someone that made me feel a little less alone. But when I started talking with a psychiatrist, I realized I could lose my regular life and go into foster care if I kept telling my secrets, so I tried to just think happy thoughts and act like I didn't have any real problems.

But my anger and thoughts of suicide didn't go away.

One day my brother was cursing a girl on the street, and I thought he was cursing me. So when he came upstairs, I started to curse him out. My mom started to yell at me and sent me to my room. I went to my room and slammed the door. My mom came in my room with a golf club and started to beat me with it. I lost my marbles. I started to yell, curse and have a tantrum, so the police were called. They thought I was suicidal, so they brought me to the emergency room. Then my moms said, "I don't want him no more." So I was placed in my first group home.

It was a good idea for me to be removed from my mother, but I hated being in a group home. (Still do.) I was so scared and pissed at the same time. But I also hoped that finally I might get help with my anger problem. It was always getting me into fights and sometimes getting me beaten up. Instead, my anger seemed to get worse.

There were so many things in group-home life that triggered my anger—the bickering, the teasing, the stealing, and the fighting. When I would get into a problem with a resident and staff would intervene, I would curse and stuff like that. Then, when I really needed help from staff, the words I'd said earlier would backfire and the staff wouldn't help me. I got moved to a lot of different group homes because of my anger.

After a while, I started thinking about suicide again. I just couldn't find a way out of my sadness and I did not trust anyone there enough to talk about my feelings with them. The sadness was not just connected with my abuse. It was also because of life in the group home. I didn't feel very safe there.

It seemed that people were always hitting me—my mom, my foster peers, sometimes even group home staff.

I even had a plan: I would either jump off the roof of my mother's building or jump in front of a subway. Then one day I made a spontaneous attempt on my life instead. It was April Fool's Day. That day, a lot of things had gone wrong. My favorite staff member was arrested due to a false allegation. I got into a fight with a friend of mine and he and his brother jumped me. I took out my frustration on myself. In the group home, with people watching, I took a knife and slit my throat. When I felt no pain, I broke a picture, took a jagged piece of glass from it, and cut my throat again.

Soon I was in the hospital. I thought I would be in there forever because of what I'd done to myself.

While I was there, I began to think about a lot of different things that had happened to me. I thought about all the abuse I'd endured in my home and at all the group homes I'd ever lived. It wasn't the pain that bothered me, it was the fact that I would always find myself in the same situation over and over again. It seemed that people were always hitting me—my mom, my foster peers, sometimes even group home staff. I'd wonder if this pattern would ever stop. What if I got married? Would I face abuse from my spouse? Would I be abused by my kids? Could I break the cycle and try not to be around people who would abuse me? Did I and my anger cause people to abuse me?

There was one patient in the hospital who was old and he couldn't talk or defend himself. He could only grunt. I didn't want to be like him. I didn't want to have the same old problems forever and end up defenseless in a hospital.

So I said to myself, "I don't care what it takes. I am going to succeed. I am going to prove to all those who hurt me in my life that I have a future!" I thought maybe I'd want to try to help other people like myself so they would not suffer what I've suffered. To do that, I needed to live.

After my discharge from the hospital, I was motivated to change my life. I started to go back to school. I did my chores and cleaned my room and showed a decent amount of respect to the staff. I started yet another program for my anger. This one paired me with a therapist who was on call 24/7.

Not all those changes stuck. I stopped going to the program after about a month. I don't always do my chores anymore, and I still get in fights. I still struggle with my anger and sometimes when I think about my past, I just want to die. My anger still gets me moved around a lot, and recently I've been running away pretty frequently. But I do feel a little more motivated to not really slip up since I tried to kill myself. I guess that showed me how serious my anger is, and I feel determined to not let that happen again.

Still, I don't know what needs to happen for me to get a firm grip on my anger and emotions. I've been in a lot of programs, and not all of them have had much of an influence on me or my anger. I think the ones that helped the most were the ones where I had a good relationship with the staff there.

I guess my anger problem is the kind of thing that takes a long time to deal with. For now, I try to focus on the positive in my life, and I try not to think about my problems too much. When that doesn't work, I tell myself that if I give in to the stupidity and really lose it, then I'm letting the bullies win.

Miguel was 19 when he wrote this story.
He later earned his GED.

Rafael Manashirov

It Ain't Easy Being Hard

By Danny Ticali

When I was younger, I used to think being bad was cool. I was insecure and all those guys who were hard or tough seemed so strong and confident.

The media also began influencing what I thought I should be. I used to watch TV shows and movies that had lots of violence in them. I'd also listen to songs that would talk about beating or killing people. I wanted to be tough like that.

I can remember sitting on street corners with my so-called "homeboys" drinking beer and waiting for some trouble. All we did was sit and talk about how crazy we were and how many people we could beat up.

My memory from that time is pretty dazed, thanks to marijuana and alcohol. But I remember brief moments of fights, and other things I did that today I am not that proud of. I always considered myself a warrior, and I thought that meant that you had to be a badass.

I had a big problem with who I was. I was very angry inside. I had a lot of my own problems and I was confused. My family and I didn't talk that much. And when we did, they would tell me to be a certain way—a nice preppy boy with short hair who always dug his nose in the books.

Meanwhile, TV and music were telling me the opposite. They made me think that the average kid was a hardass guy. I thought that to be normal you had to be hard. I thought you had to hurt people and fight and hang out with the bad boys.

So I tried to be like everyone else. I tried to be hard and a hood. I wanted everyone to admire me for how strong and confident I was. I did some bad things, like steal from a few stores, and beat people down cause I didn't like the way they looked.

I remember one time I ran into this kid Johnny, who I didn't get along with. When I saw him, my friends and I began to stare at him. So he and his friend yelled, "What are you looking at?"

When we heard him loud-mouthing to us, we ran across the street yelling, "Who do you think you're talking to?" and began to beat him and his friend down.

Those kids were afraid of me and it didn't make me feel good. I felt ashamed.

I was upset afterwards, because I wasn't mad at him; I was just pissed off in general. So I went out of my way to hurt him bad just because he asked me what I was looking at.

Slowly I began to realize that acting that way didn't make me feel better; it made me feel worse. I felt like I was hiding and lying, so I began searching for myself.

It was a slow process. I started waking up to get dressed and asking myself, "What would I like to wear?" instead of, "What would my friends like?" People began to notice the changes in me, but I no longer cared what other people thought.

One day I saw a couple of people who I knew were about to jump another kid from the neighborhood. I just happened to be walking by when they started fighting with him.

Because I knew the kid and I thought he was a nice guy, I jumped in and took his back. When everyone saw that the neighborhood bad guy—me—was involved, they wanted to chill.

Those kids were afraid of me and it didn't make me feel good. I felt ashamed, because I hardly knew them and they felt they had reason to fear me. On top of that, it made me feel that when people were nice to me or gave me things, it was because they feared me, not because they liked me.

After that day, I began to carry myself differently. I gave people the benefit of the doubt before I passed judgment on them. And I gave 110% for my friends 'cause they always returned it. The kid whose back I took in that fight is still my friend to this day.

Nowadays when I read the paper and see all the violent crimes that are being committed, it makes me think how lucky I am that I'm not dead or in prison by now. Maybe I would be if I hadn't decided to change when I did. And there are so many others out there who are like I was when I was younger—not really bad, just in need of a little direction.

I've seen too many of my friends screw up their lives or die because of stupid b.s. One good friend of mine overdosed on drugs, and another one was beaten to death while walking to the store for a soda. I'm tired of saying goodbye to my friends and I'm tired of lowering them into the ground.

I know it's tough out there. There are rapists, murderers, muggers, dealers, and junkies. And none of them give a rat's ass about you; they'd be just as happy at your funeral. But this is a war and we all have to fight. We can do that by not becoming like them.

I've learned that we don't prove how tough we are by beating people up. We do it by being able to say no and think for ourselves, by being able to take it when some people start making fun of us. We have to give a damn about our lives and our futures and let that guide our actions.

Danny was 17 when he wrote this story.

Kat Morris

The Very Lonely Bully

By Avad Ratliff

One day I went into my foster brother's room and saw all kinds of games and toys. So when he came in the room, I said, "John, can I play with your games?"

"No, get out of my face—you're not a part of this family. And don't go through my stuff."

"I didn't go through your stuff," I said, grabbing him by the neck. "N-gga, I want to play with those games."

"Ouch, stop hitting me," he said. But everything I wanted, that's how I got it: "Gimme that, n-gga, I want it." In a lot of my foster homes, bullying seemed like the only way.

I was treated badly in my foster homes and missed my family, and I didn't know how to deal with being alone. I felt bad so often that I became a bully.

Ever since I first went into foster care, when I was 6, I'd been feeling angry and alone. The Administration for Children's Services took me away from my home because my father hit my mother, my mother left home to protect herself, and my father became abusive and controlling toward us kids.

The day Children's Services came, I wanted to stay with my

father because I was scared and I didn't know where I was going. The worker didn't even tell me where or why they were taking us. Then we got split up and all my brothers and sisters went their own way.

In my first foster home, I didn't see my family for a long time—about a year and a half. I felt abandoned, like I was just passed down to a family that didn't like me and treated me like a stranger. I didn't know how to express what I was feeling, so I really acted out. I snuck ice cream, made prank phone calls to the police, and acted wild.

I missed my brother, especially. All I could do was sit in the house and daydream about the good times I'd had with my brother. Thinking about him made me feel happy, but later I would miss him and feel sad. Then I didn't have anybody to comfort me. The foster family didn't seem to care if I cried or if I was mad. They only seemed to care if I damaged anything in their house.

Finally, I got to see my mother. I missed my mother so much that I didn't know how to act the day I saw her. I was running and bouncing off walls and buying out the candy store.

My mother told me that she was working on getting me back. It was all over after that. In my foster home, instead of sneaking ice cream, I would take it out and leave it on the

I couldn't make friends because I would always take my anger out on them.

table edge so it could melt and drip on the floor. I threw food behind the stove so they could get roaches. I did whatever I could to hurt them because I felt like the foster parents treated me like a butler who had to clean for them, and I didn't like it.

After that, I went home for a couple of years. At home I felt a little calmer. I had friends who lived around my way, I played basketball, and I watched movies with my mother.

But in truth, being home didn't stop me from bullying kids at school or around my way. I still felt angry from being away from home so long, and I was mad at my father for breaking up the family. I didn't care about anybody or their feelings, just mine and what I wanted.

And I soon went back into the system. This time, I went through a lot of different foster homes and group homes. I had to make new friends all over again, and I had a real hard time doing that.

I couldn't make friends because I would always take my anger out on them. I'd want to fight all the time. I lost most of my friends, and that made me feel really sad, because most of the time I didn't mean to take things out of hand. That kept me feeling guilty for a long time.

I was even more of a bully in my foster home. If the foster mother made me do things that I didn't want to do, like wash all the dishes even though other kids were home, too, I would get mad and take it out on the other foster kids.

One time this other kid, John, was getting $10 allowance because he did a lot of cleaning around the house. When Friday came I said, "Yo, John, let me hold $5?"

"No, you can't hold any of my money. Mom said not to give you none."

"I don't care, give me some money, you stingy momma's boy," I said. Then I put a bar of soap in a sock and when he went to the bathroom I beat him with it, saying, "If you tell that b-tch I will beat you in your sleep." After that I took his money every day for a couple of weeks.

He told on me, but the social worker didn't really say anything because I told her about one of my foster fathers putting soap in a sock and beating me with it, so I guess she felt sorry for me. I found that it was easy to manipulate people.

But I felt lonely inside. To keep from feeling attached to any of my foster parents, I stopped myself from trusting people. I shut everyone out of my life. When I didn't have anybody to talk to, it didn't feel good. As a matter of fact, I felt like I was the saddest person in the world.

Holding everything inside and not talking to anybody made my sadness turn to anger. I started to feel angry every time my family visited because I didn't want them to leave me. I wanted to go home with them. Visiting my family and then having to go back to the foster homes was even harder. Between those times I was not happy at all.

When I was 12, I ended up in a residential treatment center, and that's where I learned how to talk to someone and trust someone. That helped me get a lot of problems off my chest, which helped me to stop getting mad and taking it out on my friends.

My mentor, Tammy, was 22 and lived in New Jersey. She came from a wealthy family, and she was never in foster care. But she was a good mentor to me for about five years.

We met on the campus football field one day when all the mentors came to play with us. We were all playing when another guy squeezed my damn ribs and I dropped the ball. We started fighting.

The staff tried to restrain me. My mentor came at the right moment. We sat down and talked about why I punched him and what happened. She calmed me down and from there on I liked her.

Tammy was real nice. She took me out, helped me with schoolwork and taught me a little bit of Chinese. Most of all she always listened to me and let me talk to her about my problems. She never tried to make me talk, she never tried to change me, and she never made it seem like my past was my fault. When I got in trouble, Tammy gave me the benefit of the doubt. That helped me trust her.

She also kept our conversations confidential. I feel that the only way you know if you can trust somebody is if you tell them a secret, so one time I told her that I missed my family and I was going to run away to my real home. She didn't tell any doctors or any social workers, she just talked to me and gave me a lot of advice and solutions to my problems.

From then on I trusted her and I learned a lot from her. Every time she came to the campus Tammy took me out. We went to the movies a lot, and on Thanksgiving she took me to her mother's house in New Jersey where I got to meet her family.

Her family was mad cool. At their house, I ate some home-made Chinese food and played a lot of board games—Monopoly, Life, spades—everything. I had a lot of fun.

Most of all, my mentor taught me how to calm down. If I got mad, she would hold me and let me explain what happened. Her hugs were what did it for me. I'd never had a hug when I was in the residential center.

Tammy also taught me how to be the bigger man. I was the type of person who thought, "If you want to fight, let's go." I didn't waste any time. If she saw me about to fight, she would say, "Put your hands down," and, "If he hits you, you're right and he's wrong." Then she would ask me. "Which one is better?" Before you know it, I grew out of fighting, because it started to seem childish to me. I started to see that what I was doing was wrong, like bullying and being disrespectful and selfish.

Tammy helped me get closer to my mother, too. She knew I missed my family and used to let me call my family when we hung out. Sometimes she took me to my house and let me see my mother.

My mother also proved that she was sticking with me. One time when I was in the residential center, I was getting bullied by the staff and some of the residents. My mother came there and shut all that down. That helped me a lot.

My mother is young and beautiful, with jet black hair and pretty eyes (that's for those millionaires out there). She's sweet and giving. She often sat me down and talked to me about how to act in school. She also told me, "Call me if you need anything."

The best thing that my mother did, though, was sit me down and explain to me why I'd been in foster care when I was little. She told me that after she left my father and we went into foster care, the system wouldn't let us go home to her unless she had an apartment and a job. That was hard, so it took a while.

I still felt upset that we had spent so much of our lives apart, but I started to feel better because I finally knew it wasn't my fault and that it wasn't my mother's fault either.

My mentor taught me how to calm down. If I got mad, she would hold me and let me explain what happened.

Knowing that my mother fought like hell to get me out of foster care felt good. But my mother also told me that there's going to be times when she can't help me, like when I'm on the campus, fighting and getting in trouble. My mother taught me that it wouldn't help me to blame her, myself, or anyone else for what I'd been through. Knowing that helped me get closer to people without blaming them for my problems.

With the help of my mentor and my mom, I started to be able to turn my life around a little bit. They taught me that when I throw away friendships, I have nobody to talk to. Then I hold my problems inside and just feel worse.

Once I started to taste how it felt to have friends, I didn't want to give them up. I had to learn how to do things differently, like not argue over petty stuff, or play a fair basketball game and control my anger on the court. I also learned how to be patient by giving people at least three chances before I started to get mad. When I got that down pat, my frustration lessened.

My staff and other people who knew me noticed the change. I felt good. Finally, I didn't feel like I had to bully kids. It felt kind of strange not being angry, but it wasn't something that I wanted back.

As I learned how to control my anger, I realized that I had things to look forward to in my life, like basketball, spades and chess. So when I got mad I didn't stay stuck on my anger.

Now I feel I'm in a good place in my life. I still don't completely trust people. Most of the friends I've made are really acquaintances. But I made one close friend in my residential treatment center who is still my friend today. When I went home, it turned out he lived right next to me. We chill a lot and watch over each other. He's more like my brother than my friend.

I hang out with my family more and I feel closer to them than I did growing up. Now I just need to find me a nice woman who lives far away from me (in a nicer place) and chill. That's my solution to staying out of trouble.

Avad was 22 when he wrote this story.

Stephanie "Meadow" Kunar

Vicious Cycles

By Miguel Ayala

Growing up, I felt so alone in this world. I never had any friends and I was bullied by just about everyone. My mom abused me at home and I think that kept me from making friends in school. I was afraid of rejection and afraid that my classmates would turn violent toward me.

Kids at school really would pick on me. I used to wear no-frills clothing, and they would say that I was poor and I got my clothing from the Salvation Army. I would think, "Why me? Why won't they leave me alone?"

Soon I started to be the bully. I started picking on others who were smaller and weaker than I was. I was pissed off and I wanted to see how it felt to pick on someone. I would say, "Hey dweeb!" or "Wassup shrimp?" Sometimes I would push the kid. In the short run I felt good because, being the tormentor, I felt a glimpse of power. But in the long run I didn't feel much better. I knew I didn't want to do to other people what my mom did to me.

Living with violence at home and abuse at school, I grew deeply depressed. I stayed to myself and one time I tried to end my life. Eventually I was removed from my mother's home and put in a group home. That's when I found out that bullying happens in foster care, too. In fact, in all the group homes I've been in, it's been a serious problem, one that isn't taken seriously enough.

In group homes, I've been bullied about my sexuality, my weight, and the fact that I take medication. Kids have called me names, hit me and put mustard, ketchup, and dish detergent on my bed linens. I have also witnessed other kids who live with me get bullied in the same way. One resident got snuffed in the face for saying something stupid. That was so painful for me to see. It made me feel like my mom was hitting me. All the staff did was say, "Don't do that."

Many youth who are abused or bullied tend to become bullies themselves.

Why are group homes full of bullies? I went to Jonathan Cohen, a therapist and the president of the Center for Social Work and Emotional Education in New York City, to answer that question. Cohen said that bullying is a form of abuse, and that too many people assume that it's harmless and normal behavior for kids, when it is actually very harmful.

Cohen said that many youth who are abused or bullied tend to become bullies themselves. He said that people who are being abused feel small and helpless and ashamed. They might feel like the abuse is their fault. Hurting someone else may make them feel a little less helpless for a while.

"No one likes to feel helpless," explained Cohen. "Bullying someone smaller than us or someone who has a disadvantage or who is different can make someone feel more powerful in the short run."

Most kids in group homes have been abused or neglected. As children, many of us were made to feel small and helpless, often by our parents. So it makes sense that a lot of kids in group homes are bullies. By hurting others, they're trying to feel better about themselves.

Also, some people who have grown up with abuse think abuse is a form of caring. "Repeated, serious abuse can cause a person to develop the upside-down idea that being close to someone else is the same as being bullied by someone else," said Cohen. "It can make you feel like it's normal to be bullied." People who have been abused in the past are more likely to be victims today, he said.

I was abused by my mom for years. I knew I didn't like being victimized by her, but I also thought it was normal. I began to accept my mother's abuse as a form of love from her. When she hit me, later she would say, "I'm sorry. I have been through so much and I just wasn't thinking straight. Please forgive me." And you know what? I did forgive her. Over and over again.

Like me, many teens who have been abused by their parents or someone else they care about have come to believe that bullying and abuse is a normal way to show love. This may make them feel like hurting the people they love, or it may make them accept abuse from someone they are close to.

Also, when someone hasn't received much attention in their lifetime—like when someone is neglected by their parents— they might feel that bullying is OK because it's a form of attention. They may think, "At least the person who's bullying me is acknowledging my presence." Victims of abuse may go as far as to seek out people who are likely to bully them.

But bullying is not a good way to feel bigger and better than someone. Nor is it a way to show or receive love from someone. Bullying is not love. It can have serious consequences, like depression, for both the victim and the bully.

"Ongoing bullying can and does make someone feel helpless and that can lead to serious depression," said Cohen. Research has also shown that children who bully other children are at risk for more violent behavior. That's why it's so important that adults pay attention to bullying, and help stop it.

But too often, said Cohen, adults do not intervene when they see or hear bullying. That happens in group homes a lot. Cohen said that if adults just sit aside and do nothing about bullying, they risk putting a child in harm's way and they risk sending the message that bullying is OK. But bullying is not OK. "Bullying is emotionally and socially toxic," said Cohen.

When a bully in a group home isn't stopped, everyone in that group home lives in fear. Especially for kids who have been removed from their homes due to abuse, living in fear of bullies is no way to live.

Miguel interviewed Dr. Cohen as a reporter for
Represent *magazine.*

Lee Samuel

How Adults Can Help

By Miguel Ayala

Research has shown that adults can significantly change the pattern of bullying. Giving consequences for bullying or stopping a problem before it escalates can and will make a difference, said therapist Jonathan Cohen, president of the Center for Social Work and Emotional Education in New York City. Here's what Cohen said adults can do to help stop bullying:

1. Get the bully help. Send the child who is bullying into some sort of psychotherapy, because this type of abuse can really mess up the bully's (and the victim's) head. Without therapy, a bully might not be able to grow out of bullying. Research has shown that bullying can lead to more violent behavior.

2. Teach the bully. Teach the bully how to pay attention to what they are feeling. Sometimes when a bully bullies, it is because they feel overwhelmed at the moment and don't know what they're feeling. If they can understand their feelings better, they can figure out what's bothering them and maybe even talk about it without taking it out on someone else.

3. Intervene. If there's a conflict, sit down with the bully and the victim and talk about the problem. Separate individuals who are arguing and try to settle the problem. If the teens live together (like in a group home), set up a system where every single day the house members will sit down and have a meeting.

Bullying is not normal behavior, and it can do great harm to both the person who bullies and the victims. But when adults intervene, they can help change the pattern of bullying. Research has proven that! Adults—especially the staff at group homes, where bullying is far too common—need to stop sitting by when bullying happens. They need to stand up and make a difference. Help us break the pattern of bullying and being bullied that runs in many of our lives.

Townsend Press

The Bully

With a cold November wind stabbing through his jacket, Darrell Mercer took one last walk with his best friend, Malik Stone.

"Man, I can't believe you're movin' to California tomorrow," Malik said. "I just can't believe I won't see you no more."

Darrell shook his head. He could not believe it either. In just a few hours, he would leave the only neighborhood he had ever known in his fifteen years. Soon his street, his school, and every friend he had in the world would be thousands of miles away. Thinking about what was ahead of him, Darrell felt like a man going to his own hanging.

"I'll miss you, man," Darrell said, his voice wavering. The boys had known each other since first grade at Harrison School on 44th Street. Their neighborhood was definitely not one of Philadelphia's best. Most of the buildings were old and decaying, and graffiti covered just about every one. Some houses were

Here's the first chapter from *The Bully*, by Paul Langan, a novel about teens facing difficult situations like the ones you read about in this book. *The Bully* is one of many fiction books in the Bluford Series™ by Townsend Press.

vacant, and a few had broken windows. Abandoned cars rusted along many streets, and occasionally local newscasts would run a story about city crime and feature this area as an example. To many people, the neighborhood was trouble, but to Darrell and his friends, it was home. True, there were guys selling drugs on street corners. But there were also good kids like Malik, Big Reggie, and Mark. Because of them, Darrell had never felt alone.

Inside the rundown homes that lined Darrell's block, there were always people to turn to in times of trouble. Across the street was old Mr. Corbitt, who sat on his porch each day and waved at everyone who passed by. And in the corner house was Mrs. Morton. She made sweet-potato pie for people in the neighborhood, especially Darrell and his mother.

"This'll help you grow," Mrs. Morton would say whenever she left a pie at their apartment. It never seemed to work, but Darrell didn't mind because the pies were delicious.

Darrell had always been short for his age. At fifteen years old, he was just under five feet. He was also skinny, without a respectable muscle in his small body. Back in September, Darrell had dreaded starting Franklin High, but his friends were right there with him. If anyone picked on Darrell during those first weeks of school, they had the other guys to deal with too. But all that was changing.

Darrell was moving to California two months after the school year had begun. It was the first day of high school all over again, only this time Darrell did not have his friends to protect him. Darrell did not admit it to anyone, but he was scared.

"Want a cheesesteak?" Malik asked when they came to Sal's Steaks.

"I guess," Darrell said. Sal made the best cheesesteaks in the neighborhood, or maybe in the entire city. They were loaded with gobs of dripping cheese and just the right amount of fried onions.

"This one's on me," Malik said, a crack in his voice. Physically, Malik was the opposite of Darrell. He was six feet tall with big muscular shoulders. Although he was just a freshman, Malik had already earned a position on the Franklin High School varsity football team. Ever since they were young boys, Darrell was thankful that he was Malik's friend because nobody messed with Malik or his friends. Watching Malik return with the steaks, Darrell felt a wave of sadness sweep over him.

"This is our last cheesesteak together," Malik said, handing one to Darrell.

"Thanks, Malik," Darrell said. Normally, he would devour the cheese-steak quickly, but now, for the first time he could remember, he felt as if he could not eat. His throat seemed to close up on him. It isn't fair, he thought. Why did things happen this way? Why did he have to leave his home and his best friends? And why, of all times, did it have to be in the middle of his first year of high school? He knew why. His mother had explained it many times, but she could not change how he felt. Realizing he would hurt Malik's feelings if he did not accept his gift, Darrell forced the cheesesteak down his throat. He knew it would be the last meal he would ever have with his friend.

The boys continued walking down the darkening street. Every storefront was painful for Darrell to see. He knew he would not be back to the old neighborhood again, at least not for a long time. He glanced across the street at the old grocery store. Today it looked warm and inviting, even though the owners charged too much for meats, and the fruits and vegetables were not always fresh. At the corner, they passed the Laundromat where his mother did her wash. A black mechanical rocking horse stood next to the door so parents could entertain their children while waiting for the laundry to dry. Once, Darrell and Malik gave coins to a little neighborhood kid so he could ride.

"Remember when Rasheed took four rides on our money?" Darrell asked.

"Yeah," Malik said glumly.

It was dark now. Mom had asked Darrell to be home early.

The bus was leaving at 5:15 the next morning.

Darrell looked down at the emerald-green shards of a shattered beer bottle glistening in the street light. "I guess I gotta go now, Malik," he said heavily. "I gotta go home."

Home. What a mockery that word was now, Darrell thought. Home was an empty apartment with boxes in the middle of the floor, packed for the move to California. Mrs. Morton was handling the shipping for them.

"You been a real brother to me," Darrell said. "I. . .I love you, man," Darrell blurted, his voice melting into embarrassing sobs.

Malik grabbed Darrell and gave him a bear hug. For a second, Darrell's face was jammed into Malik's shirt. Then the two separated, and, without a word, started walking in opposite directions. After a few steps, Darrell began to run.

"It's not fair!" he yelled, as he sprinted through the dark. He felt as if he were being robbed, that things were being taken from him that he could never replace.

Sure, Malik would miss him, Darrell thought, but Malik was big, and he had tons of friends. Darrell was sure Malik would be fine without him.

But Darrell was not so certain about his own future. The days ahead stretched out before him like a dark road filled with dangerous shadows. It would be like the summer Mom sent him to a camp for inner-city kids. The camp director promised Darrell and his mother that he would experience adventures in the outdoors away from the dangers of the city. What Darrell ended up experiencing was torment from a kid who wanted nothing more than to make anyone weaker than him feel as miserable as possible.

The kid's name was Jermaine, and his favorite activity was torturing Darrell . He pushed Darrell into the lake. He dropped worms into Darrell's ice cream. He put laxative in Darrell's pudding, making him sick for two days. During the whole time at camp, Darrell remained silent about Jermaine. What choice did he have? He knew he did not stand a chance against Jermaine in a fight, and he knew if he told one of the adults, Jermaine would retaliate the next time no one was watching. But the biggest reason Darrell never said anything to anyone was that he was ashamed of being so helpless. At least if he kept everything to himself, no one else would know how pathetic he was. Lately, whenever Darrell thought about California, he imagined some kid like Jermaine waiting for him. Or maybe several Jermaines. And nobody would be there to help him. Not Malik. Not anyone.

As Darrell walked down the alley towards his apartment, a stray cat greeted him. It purred and rubbed its face against his calf, looking up at him with radiant green eyes.

"This is it, Max," Darrell said, petting the cat's soft gray fur. "Your last pet from me. Goodbye, Max." The cat circled his legs.

Darrell and his mother had lived in the apartment for six years. Before that, they lived in a small house. Darrell's father was with them then, but he was killed in a car accident. After his death, Darrell's mother got a job as a clerk for an insurance agency, and they moved to the apartment.

For years, everything had been fine, but then in August a larger insurance company bought out the agency where Darrell's mother worked. To save money, the company eliminated her job along with hundreds of others. For a while, she tried to find work nearby that would pay her enough to support the two of them, but the only jobs she could find were in fast-food restaurants. Then in October, Darrell's Uncle Jason, her brother, called and offered her a job in California paying twice what she could make in their neighborhood. Darrell understood why his mother chose to take the job, but he did not like her decision. *I wish he never would have called*, Darrell thought as he walked up the steps to the apartment.

"Hi, baby," his mother said as she opened the door.

Darrell tried to hurry to his room and shield his face from his mother. He did not want her to notice he had been crying.

"Are you okay?" she asked, reaching an arm out to comfort him.

"I'm fine," Darrell said, wishing she would leave him alone. He felt bad enough without his mom fussing over him.

"Oh, baby, I know how hard it is for you to leave your friends, especially in the middle of the school year. It hurts me so much to be doing this to you. If there was any other way . . ."

"It's okay," Darrell replied.

"You know if I hadn't gotten laid off—"

"Mom, I'm telling you, it's okay," Darrell insisted.

"Your Uncle Jason promising me that job in California seemed like a godsend. I got no choice," she said, putting her hand on his shoulder.

He had heard it all before, and he knew it was true. It only made Darrell angrier knowing his mother was right. If she were doing this for some selfish reason, then he could be mad at her, and it would almost feel better. "Mom, stop callin' me 'baby,' okay?"

Darrell escaped to his bedroom and sat on the bed he would use one more night. His suitcase sat alone in the middle of the floor, ready for the morning. The room where he once felt so comfortable, his cave, was no more. All his posters had been stripped from the walls.

Sitting in the dark room by himself, Darrell wanted to do something crazy, anything to avoid moving away fro m home. *Maybe I could run away tonight and hide in one of those empty warehouses on 35th Street*, he thought. But then he remembered his mother. There was no way he would put her through that. Instead, he stretched out on his bed and stared at the ceiling, waiting for the day to arrive.

In the morning, just before sunrise, Darrell and his mother grabbed their two suitcases and climbed aboard the westward-bound bus. Darrell stared out the window as his neighborhood passed by him for the last time. His mother talked non-stop in a nervous monologue. Darrell paid little attention.

"Darrell, just give it a chance. You might like California. Uncle Jason said our new neighborhood is much nicer than here. He said the houses are well kept, and we'll be close to the stadium, and you can see baseball and football games."

Darrell closed his eyes and resolved to hate California no matter what anybody said.

"Jason also said the school you'll be going to is pretty new. It's an old neighborhood, but the school is only about fifteen years old. It's called Bluford High. It's named for an African American astronaut," his mother went on.

Darrell closed his eyes and said nothing. He knew his silence would hurt his mother's feelings. But he could not help it. Nothing she could say would convince him that he'd like California.

"Oh, honey," she added, "if you'd just give it a chance."

Darrell sank deeper into his seat.

"I hated to leave my friends too, Darrell," she continued. "I made some wonderful friends at the office and on our street, and I won't know anybody in California either except for my brother and his family."

It's different with you, Mom, Darrell thought. *You make friends easily. I'll be in class with kids who've gone through middle school together and had two months in high school to get used to each other. They'll see this kid from Philadelphia who looks twelve years old, and I'm in for it.* Yet he said nothing. He did not feel like explaining things to his mother. She would only worry about him even more.

"Just put a big, friendly smile on your face your first day there, honey, and by the end of the day you'll have at least one nice friend," she said.

Maybe that worked in first grade when everybody was wearing name tags and kids hadn't learned to be mean to each other yet, Darrell thought. But kids learn fast. By third grade, Darrell was glad he had Malik, Big Reggie, and Mark.

But now, he wouldn't have anybody.

Everything Darrell knew and loved was gone. And though she meant well, his mother had no idea how hard it was to be the new kid in school, especially one who is smaller than everyone else.

Darrell remembered that his Uncle Jason was well over six feet tall. A few years ago, he came to Philadelphia to visit, and he looked at then twelve-year-old Darrell and said in a booming voice, "Will you look at that boy? Why is he so skinny? Nobody in our family was ever that small at his age! Jackie, ain't you feedin' him enough?"

His mother seemed defensive. "Oh, he'll hit his growth spurt anytime now," she said, "He'll shoot up like a spring weed. Then you won't even recognize him, Jason."

Remembering that conversation, Darrell could only think one thing—his mother was wrong.

She refused to accept the truth, Darrell thought. And the truth was that he was still a short, underweight kid, and all the hopes and smiles in the world were not going to change that.

Darrell gazed out the window while the bus raced farther and farther fro m his home. A feeling of dread weighed heavily on him as the sun crawled slowly into the sky.

The Bully, a Bluford Series™ novel, is reprinted
with permission from Townsend Press. Copyright © 2002.

Want to read more? This and other *Bluford Series*™
novels and paperbacks can be purchased for $1 each at
www.townsendpress.com. Or tell an adult (like your teacher)
that they can receive copies of *The Bully* for free if they order a
class set of 15 or more copies of *Sticks and Stones*. To order, visit
www.youthcomm.org or call 212-279-0708 x115.

Teens:
How to Get More Out of This Book

Self-help: The teens who wrote the stories in this book did so because they hope that telling their stories will help readers who are facing similar challenges. They want you to know that you are not alone, and that taking specific steps can help you manage or overcome very difficult situations. They've done their best to be clear about the actions that worked for them so you can see if they'll work for you.

Writing: You can also use the book to improve your writing skills. Each teen in this book wrote 5-10 drafts of his or her story before it was published. If you read the stories closely you'll see that the teens work to include a beginning, a middle, and an end, and good scenes, description, dialogue, and anecdotes (little stories). To improve your writing, take a look at how these writers construct their stories. Try some of their techniques in your own writing.

Reading: Finally, you'll notice that we include the first chapter from a Bluford Series novel in this book, alongside the true stories by teens. We hope you'll like it enough to continue reading. The more you read, the more you'll strengthen your reading skills. Teens at Youth Communication like the Bluford novels because they explore themes similar to those in their own stories. Your school may already have the Bluford books. If not, you can order them online for only $1.

Resources on the Web

We will occasionally post Think About It questions on our website, www.youthcomm.org, to accompany stories in this and other Youth Communication books. We try out the questions with teens and post the ones they like best. Many teens report that writing answers to those questions in a journal is very helpful.

How to Use This Book in Staff Training

Staff say that reading these stories gives them greater insight into what teens are thinking and feeling, and new strategies for working with them. You can help the staff you work with by using these stories as case studies.

Select one story to read in the group, and ask staff to identify and discuss the main issue facing the teen. There may be disagreement about this, based on the background and experience of staff. That is fine. One point of the exercise is that teens have complex lives and needs. Adults can probably be more effective if they don't focus too narrowly and can see several dimensions of their clients.

Ask staff: What issues or feelings does the story provoke in them? What kind of help do they think the teen wants? What interventions are likely to be most promising? Least effective? Why? How would you build trust with the teen writer? How have other adults failed the teen, and how might that affect his or her willingness to accept help? What other resources would be helpful to this teen, such as peer support, a mentor, counseling, family therapy, etc.

Resources on the Web

From time to time we will post Think About It questions on our website, www.youthcomm.org, to accompany stories in this and other Youth Communication books. We try out the questions with teens and post the ones that they find most effective. We'll also post lesson for some of the stories. Adults can use the questions and lessons in workshops.

Teachers and Staff:
How to Use This Book in Groups

When working with teens individually or in groups, using these stories can help young people face difficult issues in a way that feels safe to them. That's because talking about the issues in the stories usually feels safer to teens than talking about those same issues in their own lives. Addressing issues through the stories allows for some personal distance; they hit close to home, but not too close. Talking about them opens up a safe place for reflection. As teens gain confidence talking about the issues in the stories, they usually become more comfortable talking about those issues in their own lives.

Below are general questions that can help you lead discussions about the stories, which help teens and staff reflect on the issues in their own work and lives. In most cases you can read a story and conduct a discussion in one 45-minute session. Teens are usually happy to read the stories aloud, with each teen reading a paragraph or two. (Allow teens to pass if they don't want to read.) It takes 10-15 minutes to read a story straight through. However, it is often more effective to let workshop participants make comments and discuss the story as you go along. The workshop leader may even want to annotate her copy of the story beforehand with key questions.

If teens read the story ahead of time or silently, it's good to break the ice with a few questions that get everyone on the same page: Who is the main character? How old is she? What happened to her? How did she respond? Etc. Another good starting question is: "What stood out for you in the story?" Go around the room and let each person briefly mention one thing.

Then move on to open-ended questions, which encourage participants to think more deeply about what the writers were feeling, the choices they faced, and they actions they took. There are no right or wrong answers to the open-ended questions. Open-ended questions encourage participants to think about how the themes, emotions and choices in the stories relate to their own lives. Here are some examples of open-ended questions that we have found to be effective. You can use variations of these questions with almost any story in this book.

—What main problem or challenge did the writer face?

—What choices did the teen have in trying to deal with the problem?

—Which way of dealing with the problem was most effective for the teen? Why?

—What strengths, skills, or resources did the teen use to address the challenge?

—If you were in the writer's shoes, what would you have done?

—What could adults have done better to help this young person?

—What have you learned by reading this story that you didn't know before?

—What, if anything, will you do differently after reading this story?

—What surprised you in this story?

—Do you have a different view of this issue, or see a different way of dealing with it, after reading this story? Why or why not?

Credits

The stories in this book originally appeared in the following Youth Communication publications:

"Fashion Un-Conscious," by Nadishia Forbes, *New Youth Connections*, March 1999

"I Showed My Enemies—And Hurt My Friends, Too," by Elie Elius, *New Youth Connections*, September/October 1998

"The Walking Flame," by Eric Green, *Represent*, March/April 2009

"Fortress of Solitude," by Anonymous, *New Youth Connections*, April 2009

"Feeling Different," by Isiah Van Brackle, *New Youth Connections*, November 2006

"Learning to Love My Hair, by Charlene George, *Represent*, May/June 2008

"Gay on the Block," by Jeremiyah Spears, *Foster Care Youth United*, January/February 2000

"Standing My Ground," by Xavier Reyes, *Foster Care Youth United*, November/December 1993

"Nasty Girls," by Alice Wong, *New Youth Connections*, November 2002

"Caught Between Two Colors," by Shaniqua Sockwell, *Foster Care Youth United*, January/February 1994

"Sticks and Stones," by Yen Yam, *New Youth Connections*, December 1999

" 'Can I Holla Atcha?' " by Allajah Young, *New Youth Connections*, December 2001

"Karate Killed the Monster Inside Me," by Robin Chan, *New Youth Connections*, November 1996

"Bad Boy Gets a Conscience," by Anonymous, *New Youth Connections*, April 2001

"Releasing My Rage," by Miguel Ayala, *Foster Care Youth United*, July/August 2002

"It Ain't Easy Being Hard," by Danny Ticali, *New Youth Connections*, November 1993

"The Very Lonely Bully," by Avad Ratliff, *Represent* July/August 2004

"Vicious Cycles," by Miguel Ayala, *Foster Care Youth United*, May/June 2003

"How Adults Can Help," by Miguel Ayala, *Foster Care Youth United*, May/June 2003

About
Youth Communication

Youth Communication, founded in 1980, is a nonprofit youth development program located in New York City whose mission is to teach writing, journalism, and leadership skills. The teenagers we train become writers for our websites and books and for two print magazines, *New Youth Connections*, a general-interest youth magazine, and *Represent*, a magazine by and for young people in foster care.

Each year, up to 100 young people participate in Youth Communication's school-year and summer journalism workshops where they work under the direction of full-time professional editors. Most are African American, Latino, or Asian, and many are recent immigrants. The opportunity to reach their peers with accurate portrayals of their lives and important self-help information motivates the young writers to create powerful stories.

Our goal is to run a strong youth development program in which teens produce high quality stories that inform and inspire their peers. Doing so requires us to be sensitive to the complicated lives and emotions of the teen participants while also providing an intellectually rigorous experience. We achieve that goal in the writing/teaching/editing relationship, which is the core of our program.

Our teaching and editorial process begins with discussions

between adult editors and the teen staff. In those meetings, the teens and the editors work together to identify the most important issues in the teens' lives and to figure out how those issues can be turned into stories that will resonate with teen readers.

Once story topics are chosen, students begin the process of crafting their stories. For a personal story, that means revisiting events in one's past to understand their significance for the future. For a commentary, it means developing a logical and persuasive point of view. For a reported story, it means gathering information through research and interviews. Students look inward and outward as they try to make sense of their experiences and the world around them and find the points of intersection between personal and social concerns. That process can take a few weeks or a few months. Stories frequently go through ten or more drafts as students work under the guidance of their editors, the way any professional writer does.

Many of the students who walk through our doors have uneven skills, as a result of poor education, living under extremely stressful conditions, or coming from homes where English is a second language. Yet, to complete their stories, students must successfully perform a wide range of activities, including writing and rewriting, reading, discussion, reflection, research, interviewing, and typing. They must work as members of a team and they must accept individual responsibility. They learn to provide constructive criticism, and to accept it. They engage in explorations of truthfulness, fairness, and accuracy. They meet deadlines. They must develop the audacity to believe that they have something important to say and the humility to recognize that saying it well is not a process of instant gratification. Rather, it usually requires a long, hard struggle through many discussions and much rewriting.

It would be impossible to teach these skills and dispositions as separate, disconnected topics, like grammar, ethics, or assertiveness. However, we find that students make rapid progress when they are learning skills in the context of an inquiry that is personally significant to them and that will benefit their peers.

When teens publish their stories—in *New Youth Connections* and *Represent*, on the web, and in other publications—they reach tens of thousands of teen and adult readers. Teachers, counselors, social workers, and other adults circulate the stories to young people in their classes and out-of-school youth programs. Adults tell us that teens in their programs—including many who are ordinarily resistant to reading—clamor for the stories. Teen readers report that the stories give them information they can't get anywhere else, and inspire them to reflect on their lives and open lines of communication with adults.

Writers usually participate in our program for one semester, though some stay much longer. Years later, many of them report that working here was a turning point in their lives—that it helped them acquire the confidence and skills that they needed for success in college and careers. Scores of our graduates have overcome tremendous obstacles to become journalists, writers, and novelists. They include National Book Award finalist Edwidge Danticat, novelist Ernesto Quinonez, writer Veronica Chambers and *New York Times* reporter Rachel Swarns. Hundreds more are working in law, business, and other careers. Many are teachers, principals, and youth workers, and several have started nonprofit youth programs themselves and work as mentors— helping another generation of young people develop their skills and find their voices.

Youth Communication is a nonprofit educational corporation. Contributions are gratefully accepted and are tax deductible to the fullest extent of the law.

To make a contribution, or for information about our publications and programs, including our catalog of over 100 books and curricula for hard-to-reach teens, see www.youthcomm.org

About The Editors

Hope Vanderberg was the editor of *New Youth Connections*, Youth Communication's magazine by and for New York City teens, from 2004 to 2008.

Prior to working at Youth Communication, Vanderberg specialized in science journalism and environmental education. She was an editor at Medscape.com, a medical website, wrote articles for *Audubon* and *The Sciences* magazines, and taught children and teens at environmental education centers in California and Texas. She has also worked as a field biologist, studying bird behavior in Puerto Rico.

She has a master's degree in science and environmental journalism from New York University and a bachelor's degree from Earlham College. She is currently a freelance editor.

Keith Hefner co-founded Youth Communication in 1980 and has directed it ever since. He is the recipient of the Luther P. Jackson Education Award from the New York Association of Black Journalists and a MacArthur Fellowship. He was also a Revson Fellow at Columbia University.

Laura Longhine is the editorial director at Youth Communication. She edited *Represent*, Youth Communication's magazine by and for youth in foster care, for three years, and has written for a variety of publications. She has a BA in English from Tufts University and an MS in Journalism from Columbia University.

More Helpful Books
From Youth Comunication

The Struggle to Be Strong: True Stories by Teens About Overcoming Tough Times. Foreword by Veronica Chambers. Help young people identify and build on their own strengths with 30 personal stories about resiliency. (Free Spirit)

Starting With "I": Personal Stories by Teenagers. "Who am I and who do I want to become?" Thirty-five stories examine this question through the lens of race, ethnicity, gender, sexuality, family, and more. Increase this book's value with the free Teacher's Guide, available from youthcomm.org. (Youth Communication)

Real Stories, Real Teens. Inspire teens to read and recognize their strengths with this collection of 26 true stories by teens. The young writers describe how they overcame significant challenges and stayed true to themselves. Also includes the first chapters from three novels in the Bluford Series. (Youth Communication)

The Courage to Be Yourself: True Stories by Teens About Cliques, Conflicts, and Overcoming Peer Pressure. In 26 first-person stories, teens write about their lives with searing honesty. These stories will inspire young readers to reflect on their own lives, work through their problems, and help them discover who they really are. (Free Spirit)

Out With It: Gay and Straight Teens Write About Homosexuality. Break stereotypes and provide support with this unflinching look at gay life from a teen's perspective. With a focus on urban youth, this book also includes several heterosexual teens' transformative experiences with gay peers. (Youth Communication)

Things Get Hectic: Teens Write About the Violence That Surrounds Them. Violence is commonplace in many teens' lives, be it bullying, gangs, dating, or family relationships. Hear the experiences of victims, perpetrators, and witnesses through more than 50 real-world stories. (Youth Communication)

From Dropout to Achiever: Teens Write About School. Help teens overcome the challenges of graduating, which may involve overcoming family problems, bouncing back from a bad semester, or even dropping out for a time. These teens show how they achieve academic success. (Youth Communication)

My Secret Addiction: Teens Write About Cutting. These true accounts of cutting, or self-mutilation, offer a window into the personal and family situations that lead to this secret habit, and show how teens can get the help they need. (Youth Communication)

Boys to Men: Teens Write About Becoming a Man. The young men in this book write about confronting the challenges of growing up. Their honesty and courage make them role models for teens who are bombarded with contradictory messages about what it means to be a man. (Youth Communication)

Through Thick and Thin: Teens Write About Obesity, Eating Disorders, and Self Image. Help teens who struggle with obesity, eating disorders, and body weight issues. These stories show the pressures teens face when they are confronted by unrealistic standards for physical appearance, and how emotions can affect the way we eat. (Youth Communication)

To order these and other books, go to:
www.youthcomm.org
or call 212-279-0708 x115

LaVergne, TN USA
14 September 2010
196952LV00005B/3/P